# Amish Baking at Home COOKBOOK

Hardcover Edition ISBN 978-1-4971-0515-7
Deluxe Hardcover Edition ISBN 978-1-4971-0597-3

Library of Congress Control Number: 2025936105

To learn more about the other great books from Fox Chapel Publishing, or to find a retailer near you, call toll-free 800-457-9112 or visit us at www.FoxChapelPublishing.com.

We are always looking for talented authors.

To submit an idea, please send a brief inquiry to acquisitions@foxchapelpublishing.com.

Or write to:
903 Square Street
Mount Joy, PA 17552

Printed in China

Photo credits: Lee Bottoms (food photos: 3, 4–5, 7-9, 11, 14–129, 131–147, 150–173, 176–191, 195); Naomi Stutzman Gingerich (6, 13, 130, 148, 154 [photo with father], 174, 192–194); Katie's Mercantile (126); Shutterstock.com (wabeno: story backgrounds). Photos on page 175 from *Gorgeous Quilts for Gracious Living* by Sonja Moel and Vicki Lynn Oehlke (top) and *Quilting Legacy* by Jan and Jim Shore (bottom).

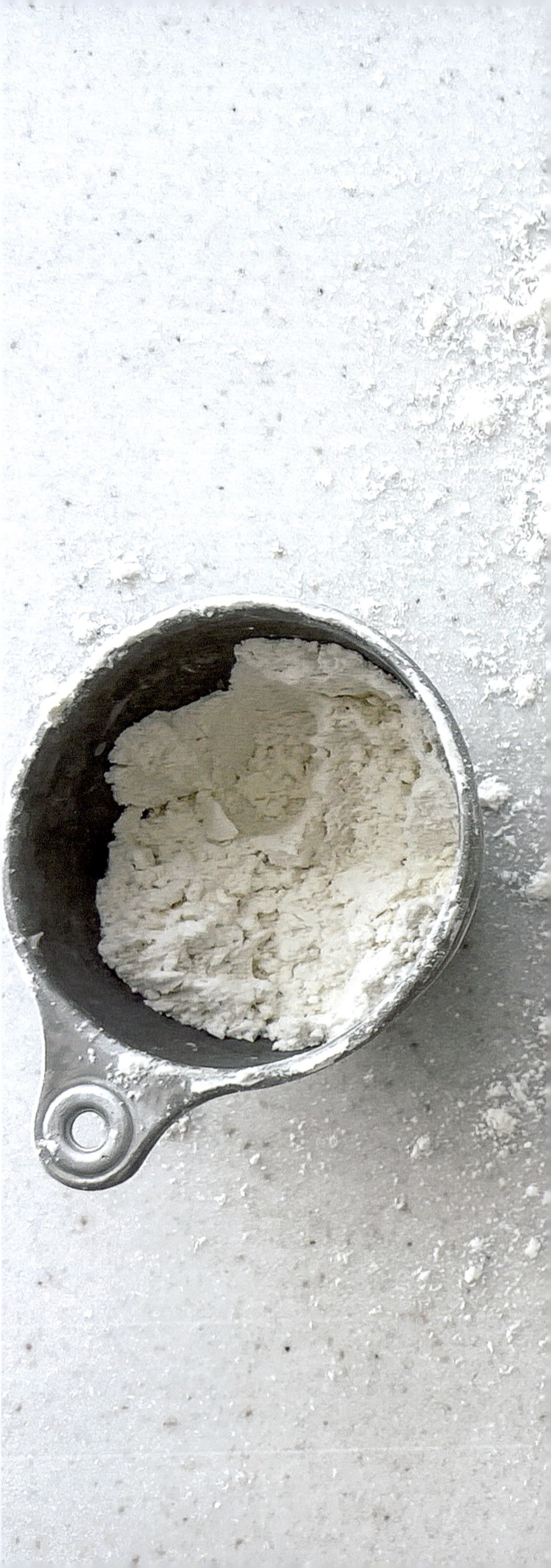

# Amish Baking at Home COOKBOOK

Recipes and Memories from My Heritage
TRADITIONS HANDED DOWN OVER GENERATIONS

— Naomi Stutzman Gingerich —

FOX CHAPEL
PUBLISHING

# Contents

87

187
64
39
120
144

# From the Fields of Holmes County, Ohio to a French-Style Café in North Carolina

Growing up in the Amish and Mennonite culture, I learned the value of good food and family traditions at a young age. Sitting at my grandmother Frannie's table, I appreciated the simplicity of apple butter toast (Slow-Cooked Apple Butter on page 187) or Mayonnaise Cake (page 53) with the thinnest glaze of brown sugar frosting. From my mother, Esther, I inherited the love of baking pies and came to crave the smell of freshly baked bread pulled from the oven. Aunt Edna was notorious for her layer cakes, and Aunt Elizabeth made the best cookies my six-year-old self could imagine.

With all these women in my ancestry line who were excellent bakers, I came to expect the taste of home and heritage in every dessert or pastry that crossed my path. It wasn't until years later, after expanding my own culinary journey, that I decided

My Amish grandmother, Frances Stutzman (on the left) with her daughter Elizabeth (right).

My parents on their wedding day in 1940.

My parents, Andrew and Esther Stutzman.

We would set the table with Mother's Blue Willow dishes for company.

to turn it into a career. But those early traditions of homemade food and neighborliness were woven into every memory of my childhood. By the age of 12, like most Amish and Mennonite girls, I had learned to cook for 30 at a moment's notice, whether for a hungry crew of threshers helping on our dairy farm or a table full of unexpected guests. I learned how to handle hot pots, bake a turkey, make browned butter gravy, and preserve bushels of corn, apples, and peaches. I learned to set a Sunday table with Mother's Blue Willow dishes, because we always used the best for company. I learned all these things and more by working at my mother's side in the daily rhythm of life, for my father was a firm believer in "more is caught than taught."

*By the age of 12, like most Amish and Mennonite girls, I had learned to cook for 30 at a moment's notice, whether for a hungry crew of threshers helping on our dairy farm or a table full of unexpected guests.*

I caught many things in those childhood years, and the traditions of our culture became an important part of my life. The community we cultivated with friends and family provided a nurturing environment with memories galore. There were weekly trips to a farmhouse bakery for Amish cinnamon rolls straight from the oven. There were ice cream suppers with neighbors who came walking across fields with pails of home-churned goodness. There were bountiful Sunday potlucks to enjoy after hours of sitting on hard pews listening to the drone of the minister. There were apple butter stirrings and taffy pulls with aunts and uncles. And there were always daily gatherings around the table.

My father often reminded me, "The best time in your life is when your children have their feet under your dinner table." I thought it was funny then, back in the day when I wore plain dresses and a traditional cap covering errant curls. Passing bowls of food and tipping cups with my kinfolk was as sure

Our French-style café, Louie and Honey's Kitchen.

*My father often reminded me, "The best time in your life is when your children have their feet under your dinner table."*

as the sun that set over our 50 acres each night. It wasn't until later, after having children of my own, that I realized the importance of family dinners in an era where fast food threatened to crowd out home cooking. I learned to appreciate the culture of slow living that made time for sit-down dinners where everyone was present, and mealtimes were punctuated with hearty laughter and storytelling. At the core, we celebrated life over plates of food around tables with those we loved.

When I left the Mennonite church at age 23, I was determined to carry this tradition of family dinners and hospitality into my own home when my husband and I married. Over the years, my table was filled with our children and friends, and then friends of friends and eventually a long list of guests who came to dine. It was inevitable that this love of cooking and baking and feasting would one day expand beyond the walls of my home. In 2017, 10 years after our family moved to North Carolina, my oldest daughter

Gathering around the kitchen table for meals is a cherished tradition—one that reflects the simplicity of Amish life and the deep value placed on family togetherness.

and I started a bakery where guests can now enjoy a taste of our heritage as they gather around tables in our French-style café.

I've introduced Amish Cinnamon Rolls and cookies and my mother's art of crafting a delicious pie. We serve tall layer cakes just like Aunt Edna's, and I set out the Blue Willow as our Sunday best for those who come through our doors. Now, this book feels like I'm opening the door and inviting you in as a guest, too, as I share this collection of recipes from our Amish and Mennonite communities.

It seems like a reunion of sorts as I flip through the pages and see many of the contributions from family and friends. These are dishes I came to expect at every wedding, funeral, church potluck, or family get-together. Some of them are unique to our culture and others are variations of recipes Amish and Mennonite women adapted from current food trends.

I hope you feel a connection with the food and stories of my heritage. Perhaps it will bring back memories of your time in the kitchen baking alongside a grandmother or aunt. And maybe it will inspire you to pass on to the next generation the unique traditions of your family. We all have stories to tell—and what better time to share them than sitting around tables with those we love, eating a home-cooked meal?

Naomi Zingerich

We still bake tall layer cakes like Aunt Edna's at Louie and Honey's Kitchen.

# How This Book Came to Be

Writing this book has been a year-long journey of immersing myself in the world of food from my childhood. If you grew up in the Amish and Mennonite culture like me, you may recognize many of these dishes from church cookbooks, sewing circles, and recipe boxes as they make their way from one generation or friend group to the next. It's been an honor to gather many of these for future generations to remember.

I've baked a dizzying array of desserts with dishes piled on counter and sink, a table spread with scribbled notes, and my trusty iPhone in my pocket documenting everything. Through it all I've gained appreciation for my ancestors who made many of these recipes before me in an age where modern conveniences weren't present. I imagine the pride they took in preparing this food to serve their families, and, yes, how tired they were at the end of the day when the last dish was washed and put away.

In tackling these recipes from our culture, I have wrestled with updating them to my current standards of baking or to keep them as women longer ago may have made them. While I grew up learning to make things from scratch, there were some things in my mother's kitchen not generally found in mine today. Crisco®, for instance, held its firm place in the cabinet right beside the stove. (To be fair, a can of lard was there, too, often used for pie dough.) In the refrigerator, Fleischmann's® Oleo was the margarine of choice, and we were never without a fat log of Velveeta®. In the pantry, an assortment of boxed cake mixes, and cream of mushroom soups shared a shelf while the freezer always held Cool Whip®. Now I try to use as many organic ingredients as I can.

I have come to compromise on some things, but recipes that listed margarine as an ingredient I've updated to butter. And while I've made room for Crisco and boxed mixes on occasion, I will never replace the billowy lusciousness of scratch-made whipped cream with a plastic container of Cool Whip. My journey in cooking has gone through several revolutions over the years as food trends have changed, new friendships around the world have developed and the world of social media has brought new recipes into my kitchen. Through it all there is a constant, though, and that is the instruction I received at my mother's side through the many years of working with her in the farmhouse kitchen of my childhood. And for that I am deeply grateful.

Recipes in the Amish and Mennonite communities are passed down through generations, much like the precious dishes in our cabinets.

# Tips and Tools

Most Amish families still do not have electricity in their homes. They tend to mix everything by hand. You don't have to do that. These are some of the trusty tools in my kitchen that I recommend:

- A stand mixer— excellent for cakes and frostings. A hand mixer will work, too, if you don't have access to a stand mixer.
- A set of dry measuring cups, a 2-cup Pyrex® glass measuring cup, and a set of measuring spoons.
- A whisk, spatula, and wooden spoon.
- A medium saucepan for compotes and sauces.
- A set of mixing bowls in three graduated sizes.
- A 9 x 12-inch baking dish.
- A 12 x 16-inch cookie baking sheet.
- A jelly roll pan (approximately 15 x 11 inches).
- A cake turntable for frosting cakes.
- 7- or 9-inch white, coated cake rounds for layer cakes.
- 6- or 8-inch round cake pans.
- An offset cake icing spatula.
- A rolling pin (I prefer a French rolling pin for pie dough).
- 9-inch (23cm) pie pans.
- A cast iron skillet, 10–12 inches.
- A standard size 9 x 5-inch loaf pan for bread.
- A pastry brush.
- A 9-inch (23cm) square baking pan.
- Parchment paper.
- A microplane zester/grater for lemons.
- A citrus juicer.
- A sharp knife set (chef knife and paring knives).
- A glass trifle or pudding bowl.
- A sifter for confectioners' sugar.
- Cooling racks.

For ingredients, I use the following:

- **Salt:** I used fine sea salt in all the recipes, and to garnish some baked goods I used Maldon flake salt.
- **Butter:** I prefer to bake with unsalted butter so I can control the amount of salt in a recipe.
- **Milk, Cream, Yogurt:** As the child of a dairy farmer, I use milk and butter in everything. I always use whole milk and full-fat cream and yogurt. Baked goods often depend on the fat content in these items, plus it tastes better.
- **Vanilla:** My mother always kept a jar of Watkins Pure Vanilla Extract in her cupboard, and though I use a different brand now, I make sure it is pure extract and not an artificial flavor.
- **Flour:** I use locally milled organic flour for baking. It's a good feeling to know I am not using flour milled from grains which were treated with pesticides and chemicals.

Preparing wholesome food from scratch for our families comes with huge rewards, but it can feel time consuming at times. I understand we are all in different phases of life, so feel free to do what works for you. And if you need to reach for a shortcut recipe on some days, no one will judge you for that. Happy baking!

These are some of the baking essentials used for making the recipes in this cookbook. →

ANCHOR
HOCKING
1/3 CUP
1/4 CUP

# CHAPTER 1

In my years of teaching pie classes at our bakery, invariably when I ask attendees to name the influential person in their lives who baked pie, they say it was their grandmother or aunt. The older women in our lives and especially our family carry many of the traditions from past generations that are so valuable to be passed along. Pie baking is one of those traditions that, if you're lucky, you learned in your grandmother's kitchen.

My own journey with pie began as a youngster of probably three or four when I stood at the elbow of my mother as her tiny and competent hands worked out pie dough on the white enamel table she used for baking. She handed me small scraps to make my own pie in child-size tins, and I eagerly rolled and pressed the dough. Early on she taught me how to crimp the edges of her pies, and that became my job as she passed each crust along to me.

I lost interest in pie when I became a teenager, and my attention turned to cakes. Besides, my mother already made a perfect pie, so why should I be bothered to learn? I much preferred to bake the sheet cakes my father loved. It wasn't until later in life that I realized Mother wouldn't always be nearby to make pie whenever my craving arose. But then the Pillsbury® frozen crusts came to my rescue.

Several years after Mother passed away, I began thinking about opening a bakery with my oldest daughter. Being able to make a luscious pie became important to me. Thankfully, my mother-in-law is also a great pie baker, and she graciously welcomed me into her kitchen for a time of hands-on training. Under her tutelage, and with the memory of my mother's hands as she worked the dough, I perfected my rusty skills in the art of pie.

Thousands of pies later, I've learned some practical tools that will help to make a pie you can be proud of. Whether you've never made a pie or if you just want to hone your skills, I hope these tips will help you as they have helped me. Now let's bake some pie!

## • RECIPES •

# Pies

# How to Make a Pie Crust



### Ingredients

3 cups (360g) all-purpose flour
1 teaspoon (5.69g) sea salt
1¼ cups (282.5g) unsalted butter or shortening
1 large egg, beaten
5 tablespoons (73.93g) cold water
1 tablespoon (14.4g) apple cider vinegar

### Step #1: Making the Dough

**1.** In a mixing bowl, whisk your dry ingredients together. Then, cut your butter into small cubes, about ½ inch in size. Toss your butter cubes into the bowl of dry ingredients.

**2.** Mixing with your hands or a pastry cutter, begin working the butter into the flour with your fingers. Scoop down to get a handful of butter and flour and smoosh it between your fingers.

**3.** Repeat this process until your dough begins to turn from a white mixture to more of an ivory-colored mixture and becomes more damp to the touch. When the butter pieces have become smaller but still chunky and the dough sticks together when you press it in your fists, stop mixing.

**4.** Make a well in the center of your crumb mixture. Pour your liquid into the well. If you're not sure about the recipe and whether you will need all the liquid or not, it's better to not pour it in all at once. This is when you need to be careful not to overwork the dough. With a wooden spoon or a spatula, gently start folding over the dough, working from the outside of the bowl towards the center. Rotate your bowl as you go, turning the dough with your spatula as you incorporate the liquid into the crumbs. Add more of your liquid if it still seems to have pockets of dry flour. Stir until incorporated and dough starts sticking together.

**5.** Put down your spatula and with your hands, pull the dough towards you, and press it against the side of the bowl. Then, turn it out onto a tabletop or work surface.

**6.** Gather the dough together in a heap and push down gently. Fold over in half. Push down gently and fold it in half again, then form it into a ball. At this point, if the recipe calls for you to divide your dough in half, cut the dough into 2 equal parts.

**7.** Wrap your disc of dough snugly in plastic wrap. Then, press down on the dough with the palm of your hand and form it into a disc. Now it is ready to go into the refrigerator where it needs to rest for at least an hour before you roll it out.

PIES

## Step #2: Rolling Out the Dough

**1.** Remove your pie dough from the refrigerator and let it rest on the counter for about 10–15 minutes before you begin rolling it out. When the dough feels pliable (you can make an indent with your finger) it is ready to roll out. I like to roll out my dough between 2 pieces of plastic wrap. This helps me to eliminate a lot of extra flour which can make the dough stiff. Starting in the center of the disc, push down and roll out, rotating the dough with each turn. Tiny pushes, tiny turns. Turning the dough will keep it in a round pie shape.

When you have reached the halfway point in size, release your dough from both pieces of plastic wrap and lay it back down again. Cover it again with the other piece of plastic and keep rolling and turning until it reaches the desired size, about 2 inches wider than your pie plate, especially if you are using a deep-dish pan.

**2.** Remove the plastic wrap and transfer your dough into the pie pan. You can wrap the dough loosely around the rolling pin to help you transfer it, or you can fold it in half and drop it into the pan and then unfold it in the pan. With your left hand, lift the dough while your right hand pushes it snugly against the sides of the pan. Do this all the way around. Making sure your dough is tucked in snugly against the sides will help to eliminate the shrinking problem of the crust after it's baked.

If you are making a single-crust pie, you are ready to do the crimping. If you are making a double-crust pie, roll out the top crust just like you did the bottom crust and let it rest in the refrigerator until you are ready for it.

## Step #3: Crimping

**1.** Fold under the edge of the pie crust and tuck it in so that it is even with the edge of your pan. Keep scissors handy to trim off excess dough. If you are crimping a double-crust pie, take the top crust and the bottom crust together and fold them both under so they fit to the edge of your pie pan.

2. Everyone develops their own style of crimping, but here is a good way to start. Place your two index fingers on the rim of the crust in the shape of an "A" and push in the middle with your thumb. Repeat this process all the way around. Now your crust is ready for filling and baking. If you won't use the dough right away, wrap it in plastic wrap and a plastic bag and store it in your refrigerator for up to 3 days, or in your freezer for up to 2 months.

## Step #4: Par-Baking and Blind-Baking

1. Par-baking a crust means to partially bake a crust before adding the filling and continuing to bake the pie. This ensures the bottom crust will be done baking by the time the filling is done. It is especially helpful with custard or pumpkin pies since the filling only takes a short amount of time to bake. Par-baking is generally not used for fruit pies. To par-bake a crust, dock the crust all around by piercing it with the tines of a fork.

2. Line the crust with parchment paper and fill it with baking beans or ceramic pie weights to keep the crust from puffing up during the baking process. A trick I learned is to crumple the parchment paper first before putting it into your pie crust. This makes it more pliable.

3. Bake the pie crust in the oven at 425°F for about 20 minutes. Remove the pan from the oven and gently lift out the parchment paper with the weights. Reduce the oven to 375°F and bake the crust for an additional 5–10 minutes until the bottom no longer appears wet. Remove from the oven. When your filling is prepared, simply pour it into the par-baked crust and bake it in the oven per recipe instructions. The par-baked crust may also be stored in a plastic bag on your counter for up to 2 days before using.

4. Blind-baking a crust means to fully bake the bottom crust without a filling. This method is used for pies that do not require a baked filling, such as pudding or cream pies. To blind-bake a crust, dock the crust all over with the tines of a fork, then cover it with parchment paper and fill it with baking beans or ceramic pie weights. Bake at 425°F for about 20 minutes, then remove the crust from the oven and carefully lift the parchment paper and weights out of the crust. Reduce the temperature to 375°F, slide the crust back into the oven, and bake for an additional 10–15 minutes until the bottom is dry and nicely golden. Allow to cool on the counter, then fill with your favorite pie filling or store on the counter in a plastic bag for up to 2 days before using it.

# Fresh Blueberry Pie

*Folding in additional blueberries after the filling has been cooked allows the fresh taste of the fruit to be present. Every luscious bite will be bursting with whole blueberries puddled in a blueberry filling.*

**One 9-inch (23cm) baked pie crust**
**4 cups (600g) fresh blueberries**
**2 cups (300g) fresh blueberries (set aside)**
**½ cup (117.66g) water**
**3 tablespoons (21g) cornstarch**
**2 tablespoons (29.57g) water**
**⅔ cup (134.66g) white sugar**
**Juice of 1 lemon, approximately 2 tablespoons (30g)**
**1 pinch salt**
**1 tablespoon (14.25g) butter**

1. In a medium saucepan, heat the 4 cups of blueberries with ½ cup water until they begin to burst, approximately 5 minutes. Meanwhile, in a small bowl make a slurry with the cornstarch, water, lemon juice, salt, and sugar, whisking until no lumps remain. Add the slurry to the bubbling blueberries on the stove and whisk constantly until the mixture thickens and starts to boil. Allow this mixture to bubble for about 1 minute, then remove from heat and whisk in the butter. Pour into a bowl and set in the refrigerator to chill.

2. When blueberry mixture has cooled, fold in 2 additional cups of fresh blueberries and pour into a baked pie crust. Chill several hours or overnight in the refrigerator. To serve, top with whipped cream or ice cream.

# Oatmeal Pie Crust (gluten-free)

*Grandma Linda Gingerich, Millersburg, Ohio*

*Whether your diet is gluten-free or not, this crust is a delicious alternative to a regular all-butter or shortening pie crust. I like to use it with the Blackberry Cream Pie (page 21) or any version with Cream Cheese Whipped Cream (page 80) and a fruit compote.*

**1 cup (99g) organic rolled oats**
**⅓ cup (32g) almond flour**
**⅓ cup (71g) brown sugar**
**1 pinch salt**
**⅓ cup (75.33g) soft butter**

In a mixing bowl, combine the oats, flour, sugar, and salt. Mix in the soft butter with a fork or your hands until crumbly. Press onto bottom and sides of a 9-inch (23cm) pie pan. Bake at 350°F until golden brown, approximately 12–15 minutes. During the baking process, the sides of the crust may slide down, so when you remove the pan from the oven, gently push the sides of the crust back up using a measuring cup or a spoon. Cool completely and fill with your favorite cooked pie filling.

# Blackberry Cream Pie (gluten-free)

*The oat crust for this pie gives it a rustic taste and works beautifully with any berries or stone fruit. It's also a delicious gluten-free option to serve when guests come for dinner.*

One 9-inch (23cm) Oatmeal Pie Crust (page 20), baked

**Cream Cheese Filling**

8 ounces (226.8g) cream cheese
1½ cups (165g) confectioners' sugar
1½ cups (368g) heavy whipping cream
1 teaspoon (5g) pure vanilla extract

**Blackberry Topping**

2 pints fresh blackberries, about 2½-3 cups (360g)
¼ cup (58.83g) water
⅓ cup (67.33g) white sugar
1 pinch salt
1 tablespoon (7g) cornstarch
Juice of 1 lemon (about 2 tablespoons or 30g)

1. In the bowl of a stand mixer, beat the cream cheese and confectioners' sugar until creamy and well blended. Scrape the bowl with a spatula. With the mixer running on medium speed, slowly drizzle the cream against the side of the bowl until fully incorporated, then add the vanilla. Whip until the mixture forms stiff peaks. Chill in the refrigerator until you are ready to assemble the pie.

2. Heat the berries, water, sugar, and salt on the stovetop until the berries soften and release their juices. Make a slurry with the lemon juice and cornstarch, then stir into the blackberry mixture. Stir constantly until mixture thickens, bubbles, and turns clear. Remove from heat and cool completely.

**Assembly:** Pour the Cream Cheese Filling into the oat crust and cover with the blackberry topping. Chill and serve.

# Strawberry Pie

*Amish Community Cookbook*

*This classic strawberry pie has a cooked filling with additional fresh strawberries folded in after the filling has been cooled. It is featured in many Amish restaurants as a favorite during summer months.*

**One 9-inch (23cm) pie crust, baked**
**4 cups (approximately 540g) whole strawberries**
**½ cup (117.66g) water**
**3 tablespoons (21g) cornstarch**
**1 cup (202g) white sugar**
**1 tablespoon (14.25g) butter**
**1 tablespoon (15g) lemon juice**
**1 pinch salt**
**Whipped cream**

Sort the strawberries into 2 equal parts. Crush the part that has the imperfect berries. Cut the remaining berries into quarters or halves depending on size. Add the water mixed with the cornstarch to the crushed berries. Cook until thick and clear. Add the sugar, butter, lemon juice, and salt. Cool completely. Fold the reserved cut berries into the cooled filling. Pour into the baked pie crust and chill for several hours. Serve with whipped cream.

# Vanilla Crumb Pie

*Esther Miller, Mt. Hope, Ohio*

*This pie has a pre-cooked vanilla-caramel sauce that you pour into the bottom of an unbaked pie crust and then top with a generous ratio of soft crumbs. It is a favorite in many Amish restaurants.*

**One 9-inch (23cm) pie crust, unbaked**
**1 cup (165g) light brown sugar**
**⅓ cup (40g) all-purpose flour**
**2 cups (473.18g) water**
**1 cup (328g) Karo or maple syrup**
**1 large egg, well-beaten**
**1 teaspoon (4.3g) pure vanilla extract**

**Crumbs**

**1½ cups (180g) all-purpose flour**
**½ cup (82.5g) light brown sugar**
**¼ cup (56.5g) softened butter**
**1 teaspoon (5.6g) baking soda**

1. Whisk the sugar with the flour, then pour all ingredients into a medium saucepan and bring to a boil, whisking constantly. When the mixture boils, remove from the stovetop and stir in the vanilla extract. Cool to room temperature, then pour into an unbaked 9-inch (23cm) pie crust.

2. Mix the crumb ingredients together in a bowl. Top the pie with the crumbs and bake at 425°F for 10 minutes, then reduce heat to 350°F and bake for an additional 25 minutes.

# Blackberry Pie

*When the summer heat ripens juicy blackberries along hedge rows, it is the perfect time to bake this pie. It's tart and sweet, and tastes just right with a scoop of vanilla ice cream. If your berries are extra tart, just add about ¼ cup (50.5g) more sugar to the filling.*

**2 discs of pie dough, rolled out for a 9-inch (23cm) double-crust pie, unbaked**
**5 cups (approximately 700g) blackberries (fresh or frozen, drained)**
**¼ cup (28g) cornstarch**
**1 cup (202g) white sugar**
**1 tablespoon (15g) lemon juice**
**¼ teaspoon (2g) salt**
**2 tablespoons (28.25g) butter, cut into 4 chunks**
**Egg wash (1 large egg yolk mixed with 2 tablespoons [11 g] heavy cream)**

Place the blackberries into a medium-sized mixing bowl. Stir together the sugar and cornstarch, then pour over the berries. Add the lemon juice and pinch of salt, then stir all together and let it set on the counter, stirring occasionally, for about 10 minutes. When the berries start to release their juice, pour the filling into a 9-inch (23cm) unbaked pie crust, top with the chunks of butter, cover with a top crust, cut vent holes, and crimp. Brush top lightly with egg wash (not the crimped part). Chill in refrigerator for about 15 minutes prior to baking so the butter in the crust gets cold again. This will help produce a flakier crust. Bake at 425°F for 15 minutes, then reduce heat to 375°F and bake for an additional 40–45 minutes until you see the filling is bubbling in the center vent hole. Cool completely before cutting and serving.

*If the pie is getting too dark, you can decrease the heat to 350°F towards the end of the bake time or cover it loosely with aluminum foil.*

# Apple Pie

*When baking an apple pie, I like to use an assortment of apples to bring out the best flavor and texture. My favorite combinations are Granny Smith, Gala, and Honey Crisp. Other varieties I love are Arkansas Black, Pink Lady, and McIntosh.*

**2 discs of pie dough for a 9-inch (23cm) double-crust pie, unbaked**
**6 cups (654g) peeled and sliced apples (using about 7 large apples)**
**½ cup (106.5g) brown sugar, packed**
**¼ cup (99g) white sugar**
**2 teaspoons (10g) lemon juice**
**4 tablespoons (30g) all-purpose flour**
**1 pinch salt**
**1 teaspoon (1.89g) pumpkin pie spice**
**½ teaspoon (2.64g) ground cinnamon**
**Egg wash (1 egg yolk mixed with 2 tablespoons [30 g] heavy cream)**

1. In a large bowl, stir together all the ingredients until the apples are coated. Then, in a large saucepan with a lid, pour the filling into the pan and cover with a lid. Turn the heat to medium and cook the apples slowly until they are fork-tender, stirring them frequently. This takes about 25 minutes. Using this method of slow cooking in a covered pot helps the apples keep their shape after you bake them in the oven. They will not turn mushy! (Thanks to *Cooks Illustrated* for this tip.)

2. Cool the filling completely, then place into a 9-inch (23cm) pie crust and cover with a top crust. Seal and vent, then brush with egg wash. Chill in refrigerator for about 20 minutes prior to baking.

3. Bake at 425°F on a preheated pan in the oven for about 20 minutes, then reduce heat to 375°F and bake for an additional 30–35 minutes until crust is golden. Remove from the oven and sprinkle with additional white sugar if desired.

*For this pie, the filling is heated in a covered pan on the stovetop until the apples are fork-tender. It also has an unusual ingredient: pumpkin pie spice! My niece gave me this idea and it has become a favorite.*

# Coconut Oatmeal Custard Pie

*Esther Miller, Mt. Hope, Ohio*

*This is a traditional Amish recipe featuring a custard on the bottom topped with coconut which bakes into a caramelized texture. This pie benefits from a par-baked crust to ensure the bottom crust is done baking when the custard is set.*

**Two 9-inch (23cm) pie crusts, par-baked**
**1 cup (202g) white sugar**
**1 cup (165g) light brown sugar**
**1 cup (99g) oats**
**4 tablespoons (30g) all-purpose flour**
**1 cup (328g) dark Karo or maple syrup**
**6 large eggs, beaten**
**1 pinch salt**
**5 tablespoons (70g) butter, melted**
**4 cups (560g) whole milk**
**1 cup (80g) shredded unsweetened coconut**

In a large bowl, whisk the sugar, oats, salt, and flour together. Then, add the rest of the ingredients and stir together until blended. Pour into 2 par-baked pie crusts (or unbaked crusts, if you prefer). Bake at 400°F for 15 minutes, then reduce heat to 325°F and bake until done, approximately 25 more minutes. Pie should still be a little jiggly like Jell-O® when removed from the oven.

# Fresh Peach Pie

*Geneva Schlabach, Sarasota, Florida*

*Many of the Amish fruit pie recipes feature Jell-O to help as a binding agent and to add color and a pop of flavor. While I tend to make things from scratch without food dyes, this is a delicious pie that sets up beautifully and the color stays vibrant.*

**One 9-inch (23cm) pie crust, baked**
**2 cups (470.64g) water, divided**
**1 pinch salt**
**1 cup (202g) white sugar**
**One 3-ounce package (85g) Peach Jell-O**
**3 tablespoons (30g) Clear Jel® or Thermflo®**
**3 cups (500–600g) sliced peaches**
**Whipped cream, for topping**

In a medium saucepan, bring to boil 1½ cups water with 1 cup of sugar, salt, and the package of Peach Jell-O. While this is coming to a boil, make a slurry with the Clear Jel or Thermflo and ½ cup (117.66g) water. When the mixture on the stove is boiling, add the Clear Jel slurry and whisk constantly to avoid lumps. When the filling has turned translucent, remove from heat and pour into a bowl to cool. When the filling has cooled for several hours on the countertop, fold in the sliced peaches and then pour into a pre-baked pie crust. Chill thoroughly in the refrigerator for at least 4 hours, then top with whipped cream before serving.

# Chocolate Pie

*This is a chocolate pudding pie made with cocoa powder and then poured into a pre-baked pie crust and served with whipped cream. The recipe was handwritten by my mother in her beautiful script with a notification that it was given to her by a Miller cousin. I have made a few modifications, but it still carries the comforting taste I remember from family reunions.*

**One 9-inch (23cm) pie crust, baked**
**¾ cup (151.5g) white sugar**
**¾ cup (123.75g) brown sugar**
**⅓ cup (40g) cocoa powder (my favorite is Cacao Barry®)**
**½ teaspoon (2.84g) sea salt**
**¼ cup (28g) cornstarch**
**4 large egg yolks, beaten slightly**
**3 cups (732g) whole milk, divided**
**3 tablespoons (42.38g) unsalted butter**
**1 tablespoon (13g) pure vanilla extract**

In a medium mixing bowl, whisk together the sugar, cocoa powder, salt, and cornstarch. Then, add the beaten egg yolks and 1 cup (244g) of milk and whisk until smooth. In a medium saucepan, heat the remaining 2 cups (488g) of milk until steaming with bubbles around the edge. Then, whisk in the chocolate mixture and continue whisking steadily until the pudding starts to boil. Allow to boil for 30 seconds, then remove from the heat and whisk in the butter and vanilla. Pour into a bowl to cool in the refrigerator for about 1 hour, then pour into a pre-baked pie crust and chill for 4 hours before serving. Top with whipped cream, if desired.

# Shoofly Pie

*Amish Community Cookbook*

*A popular pie in Lancaster County, PA, this recipe is steeped in lore as to its origination, but most think it may have started out as a cake during the early years of our country's beginnings. This version has a delicious molasses (or sorghum) custard topped with a hefty dose of crumbs.*

**One 9-inch (23cm) pie crust, unbaked**
**1 cup (120g) flour**
**¾ cup (123.75g) brown sugar**
**1½ tablespoons (21.19g) butter**
**1 cup (340g) sorghum (or molasses)**
**1 egg, fork-beaten**
**¾ cup (176.5g) hot water**
**1 teaspoon (6g) baking soda**

1. Mix flour, brown sugar, and butter with a fork or crumble with your fingers. Reserve 1 cup of crumbs for the topping and spoon the rest evenly into the bottom of the unbaked pie shell.

2. Mix the baking soda in hot water. Whisk the beaten egg with the sorghum and then whisk in the soda/water mixture. Stir all together and pour into the pie crust. Top with remaining crumbs. Bake at 400°F for 10 minutes, then reduce heat to 350°F and bake for an additional 30 minutes. Pie is done when a 2-inch diameter in center is still a bit wobbly.

# Strawberry Hand Pies

*Makes 8–10 hand pies*

*Perfect for picnics or school lunches, these hand pies are made with a fresh strawberry pie filling and baked in the oven. Hand pies are little pockets of flaky pie dough filled with luscious fruit fillings. When strawberries are ripe in late spring, I love to make these for my family.*

- **2 discs pie dough, ready to roll out**
- **1 quart (500–600g) strawberries, washed and halved**
- **½ cup (101g) white sugar**
- **1 tablespoon (15g) lemon juice**
- **½ teaspoon (2.84g) sea salt**
- **¼ cup (58.83g) water**
- **3 tablespoons (21g) cornstarch**
- **1 tablespoon (14g) butter**
- **Egg wash (1 large egg yolk mixed with 2 tablespoons [11 g] heavy cream)**

1. Place strawberries, sugar, salt, and lemon juice in a saucepan and start to cook over medium heat. Let it boil gently for about 5 minutes to soften the berries. Meanwhile, make a slurry with the water and the cornstarch, stirring to remove any lumps. Drizzle the slurry into the strawberries on the stovetop and stir gently until mixture turns from cloudy to translucent. Boil for about 1 minute more, then remove from heat and stir in 1 tablespoon of butter. Transfer to a bowl to cool.

2. While the strawberry pie filling is cooling, you can roll out your dough into 2 large circles and cut those circles into smaller 4- or 5-inch circles. Keep a tray in the refrigerator and, as you cut out the circles, place them single layer on the tray (separate layers with parchment or wax paper).

**Assembly:** Brush the edges of one-half of each circle. Then, place 1–2 tablespoons of filling in the middle of each circle. Fold the circles in half, pinch the edges shut with your fingers, then lay the hand pie on the counter and crimp around the edges with a fork to seal completely. Cut 3 small vents in the top of each hand pie. Brush with egg wash. Chill in refrigerator for about 15 minutes prior to baking so the butter in the crust gets cold again. This will help produce a flakier crust. Bake on a parchment-lined baking tray at 375°F for 20–30 minutes until golden brown. Sprinkle hand pies generously with white sugar when you remove them from the oven.

# Glazed Peach Pie

*Amish Community Cookbook*

*The taste of fresh peaches shines in this pie. While you can top it with regular whipped cream, it is especially delicious with Cream Cheese Whipped Cream (page 80).*

**One 9-inch (23cm) pie crust, baked**
**4 cups (900g) fresh, sliced peaches**
**1 cup (202g) white sugar**
**3 tablespoons (21g) cornstarch**
**½ cup (117.66g) water**
**1 tablespoon (14.25g) butter**
**Juice of 1 lemon, approximately 2 tablespoons (30g)**
**Cream Cheese Whipped Cream (page 80), whipped cream, or ice cream**

Measure peaches into a bowl and toss with lemon juice. Take out 1 cup of peaches and crush or chop finely. Place the crushed peaches in a medium pot on the stove. Whisk together the sugar and cornstarch, then add to the peaches on the stove, along with the water. Bring to a boil while stirring constantly until mixture turns clear. Remove from the heat and stir in the butter. Pour into a glass bowl and put in the refrigerator to cool slightly. Then, stir in the remaining peaches and pour into a baked pie crust. Chill completely, at least 2 hours. Serve with Cream Cheese Whipped Cream, whipped cream, or ice cream.

# Cherry Pie

*Treasured Amish and Mennonite Recipes*

*I remember summer days on the farm when my father picked buckets and buckets of sour cherries from the tree in our backyard. Then, we would sit on the porch swing together and pit the cherries while he told stories of growing up as a child during the Great Depression. Later, Mother would bake the most delicious cherry pies, which we enjoyed with scoops of vanilla ice cream.*

**Two 9-inch (23cm) pie crusts, unbaked**
**3¾ cups (423.75g) cherries, drained, reserve some juice (fresh or frozen and thawed)**
**¼ cup (56g) of cherry juice**
**1 cup (202g) white sugar**
**3 tablespoons (40g) quick-cooking tapioca**
**½ teaspoon (2g) almond extract**
**1 teaspoon (5g) lemon juice**

Mix cherries, juice, tapioca, sugar, almond extract, and lemon juice in a bowl and let it set for 15 minutes. The 15-minute wait is crucial for the tapioca to activate in the filling. Then, pour into a 9-inch (23cm) pie crust, cover with a top crust, crimp and seal, and cut vents in top. Brush the top crust with egg wash. Chill in refrigerator for about 15 minutes prior to baking so the butter in the crust gets cold again. This will help produce a flakier crust. Bake at 425°F for 10 minutes and then reduce heat to 375°F for 45 minutes, or until juice is bubbling and turns to the consistency of syrup. Sprinkle pie with white sugar, if desired, when you remove it from the oven.

# Blueberry Hand Pies

*Makes 8–10 hand pies*

*Hand pies are little pockets of dough in the shape of a half-moon made to hold a fruit filling. They are similar in concept to fry pies, except these are baked instead of being fried in fat.*

**2 discs pie dough, ready to roll out**
**4 cups (600g) fresh blueberries**
**½ cup (117.66g) water**
**2 tablespoons (14g) cornstarch**
**2 tablespoons (29.58g) water**
**⅔ cup (134.66g) white sugar**
**Juice and zest of 1 lime or lemon**
**1 pinch salt**
**1 tablespoon (14g) butter**
**Egg wash (1 large egg yolk mixed with 2 tablespoons [11 g] heavy cream)**

1. In a medium saucepan, heat the blueberries with ½ cup water until they begin to burst, approximately 5 minutes. Meanwhile, in a small bowl, make a slurry with the cornstarch, 2 tablespoons water, citrus juice, and sugar, whisking until no lumps remain. Add the slurry to the bubbling blueberries on the stove and whisk constantly until the mixture thickens and starts to boil. Allow to bubble for about 1 minute, then remove from heat and whisk in the butter and citrus zest. Pour into a bowl to cool completely.

2. While the blueberry pie filling is cooling, you can roll out your dough in a circle for pie dough. Then, cut each large circle into smaller 4- or 5-inch circles. Keep a tray in the refrigerator and as you cut out the circles. Place them single layer on the tray (separate layers with parchment paper or wax paper).

**Assembly:** Place about 1–2 tablespoons of filling on each circle of dough, fold in half, and pinch edges to seal, then crimp with fork along edge. Place on a parchment-lined baking tray, brush with egg wash, then cut 3 small vents in the top of each hand pie. Chill them in the refrigerator while you preheat the oven. To bake, preheat the oven to 375°F. Bake hand pies for about 30 minutes until golden brown, rotating the tray halfway through bake time. Remove from oven and sprinkle generously with white sugar.

# Mom's Custard Pie

*My mother's custard pie was crave-worthy as she baked it weekly throughout my childhood and growing up years. I would cut a fat slice, cradle it in my hand, and sit on the porch swing to enjoy it, often going back for an additional slice or two. Custard pie isn't fancy, but when baked properly it has a comforting taste and velvety texture that's hard to beat.*

- One 9-inch (23cm) pie crust, unbaked
- 4 large eggs
- 1½ cups (349.50g) whole milk, divided
- 1 cup (165g) brown sugar
- 1 teaspoon (2.5g) all-purpose flour
- ½ cup (156g) sweetened condensed milk
- 1 teaspoon (4.34g) pure vanilla extract
- 1 pinch sea salt

In a blender, whiz the eggs and ½ cup (116.50g) milk for a few seconds until blended. Then, add the brown sugar and flour and whiz again until blended. In a microwave-safe measuring cup, heat 1 cup (233g) of milk and sweetened condensed milk for 3 minutes. Pour into the blender with the first mixture and then add the vanilla and salt. Whiz for several seconds one final time until mixture is blended. Pour into an unbaked 9-inch (23cm) pie crust. Bake at 410°F for 10–15 minutes, then reduce heat to 350°F and bake for an additional 25 minutes. Remove from oven while still a little jiggly in the middle. The pie will firm up as it cools.

# Mom's Pie Crust

*Michelle Gingerich, Sugarcreek, Ohio*

*This recipe is from my sister-in-law and is the recipe her Mennonite mother always uses for pie. It has an interesting ingredient of vinegar which helps to tenderize the dough and create even browning. It bakes up into a flaky and delicious crust regardless of whether you use butter or shortening.*

- 3 cups (360g) all-purpose flour
- 1¼ cups (282.5g) unsalted butter or shortening
- 1 teaspoon (5.69g) sea salt
- 1 large egg, beaten
- 5 tablespoons (73.93g) cold water
- 1 tablespoon (14.4g) apple cider vinegar

In a medium mixing bowl, mix the flour, salt, and butter together with your hands or a pastry cutter until the dough crumbs begin to stick together. In a small bowl, beat the egg and add the cold water and vinegar. Pour the egg mixture into the center of the crumb mixture and fold over with a spatula until the dough crumbs begin to stick together to form a nice dough. Don't over-mix after you add the liquid to the crumbs—mix just enough to get the dough to stick together. Form into a ball, divide dough in half, press into 2 disc shapes, wrap in plastic wrap, and refrigerate for at least 1 hour. Roll out and press into pie pans.

# Blueberry Pie

*Made from scratch with fresh blueberries, this pie is a summer classic when blueberries are abundant. Baked in a double crust, it is perfect with a scoop of ice cream.*

**Two 9-inch (23cm) pie crusts, unbaked**
**5 cups (750g) fresh blueberries**
**¾ cup (151.47g) white sugar**
**1 tablespoon (7g) cornstarch**
**1 teaspoon (5.69g) sea salt**
**1 tablespoon (15g) lemon juice**
**¼ cup (30g) all-purpose flour**
**2 tablespoons (28.26g) unsalted butter**
**Egg wash (1 large egg yolk mixed with 2 tablespoons [11 g] heavy cream)**

1. In a medium-sized mixing bowl, combine the berries, sugar, cornstarch, salt, and flour. Stir in the lemon juice and pour into a 9-inch (23cm) unbaked pie crust. Cut the butter into several chunks and sprinkle over the top of the filling, then cover with a top crust and crimp to seal the edges. Cut a vent hole in the middle of the top crust using a cookie cutter. Brush with egg wash (avoid egg wash on the crimped edge), and place the pie in the refrigerator or freezer to chill for about 10–15 minutes prior to baking.

2. Preheat the oven to 425°F. Place a baking sheet on the middle rack to preheat. When oven is ready and your pie has chilled, place the pie on the preheated baking sheet and bake for 20 minutes. Reduce the heat to 375°F, rotate the tray, and bake for another 20 minutes. Rotate the tray once more and bake for an additional 20-25 minutes. When the juice of the pie is bubbling from the vent hole and has turned to a thicker consistency like maple syrup, the pie is done. Fruit pies generally need to bake for 60-80 minutes, depending on the heat of your oven. If desired, sprinkle with white sugar when pie comes out of the oven. Let pie cool completely before cutting and serving.

# Pumpkin Pie

*Sara Mae Stutzman, Dover, Ohio*

*This is my sister-in-law's recipe and is a custard-style pumpkin pie. So velvety and delicious, it has a frothy brown top made from beaten egg whites.*

- One 9-inch (23cm) pie crust, unbaked or par-baked
- 3 large eggs, separated (save whites to add last)
- ¼ cup (50g) white sugar
- ½ cup (106.5g) brown sugar
- ¼ teaspoon (0.7g) cinnamon
- ¼ teaspoon (0.7g) allspice
- 1 tablespoon (7.5g) all-purpose flour
- ¾ cup (183.75g) pumpkin
- 1½ (366g) cups whole milk

In a medium-sized bowl, mix the egg yolks, sugar, spices, flour, and pumpkin. Whisk in the milk. In a separate bowl, beat the egg whites to a soft foam, then whisk into the pie filling. Pour the filling into a 9-inch (23cm) pie crust. Bake at 400°F for 10 minutes, then decrease heat to 350°F and bake for an additional 30-40 minutes or until done. Pie will still have a slight jiggle when removed from oven.

# Pumpkin Custard Pie

*This was my mother's go-to recipe for a pumpkin pie, and once you taste the creamy, custard-like filling, you'll know why. This creamy filling is a combination of pumpkin and custard. Par-baking the crust before adding the filling will ensure a flaky bottom crust.*

- One 9-inch (23cm) pie crust, unbaked
- ¼ cup (53.25g) brown sugar
- ¼ cup (50g) white sugar
- 2 large eggs, separated
- ½ cup (122.5g) pumpkin puree
- 1 tablespoon (7.5g) all-purpose flour
- ½ teaspoon (2.84g) sea salt
- ½ teaspoon (1.49g) pumpkin pie spice
- 2 tablespoons (30g) maple syrup
- 2 tablespoons (28.26g) unsalted butter, melted
- 1¼ cups (320g) evaporated milk

Beat 2 egg whites to medium peaks and set them aside. In the bowl of a stand mixer, combine the sugars, egg yolks, and pumpkin puree. Whisk together the flour, salt, and spice, then add to the pumpkin mixture. Beat in the maple syrup and the milk. Lastly, fold in the egg whites. Pour into an unbaked pie crust. Bake at 400°F for 10 minutes, then reduce the temperature to 350°F and bake for an additional 30 minutes. Pie should still be jiggly when removed from the oven.

# Apple Butter Pie

*Treasured Amish and Mennonite Recipes*

*This creamy pie flavored with warm spices and apple butter is a perfect dessert option for an autumn gathering.*

**One 9-inch (23cm) pie crust, unbaked or par-baked**
**½ cup (138.48g) apple butter**
**2 large eggs**
**½ cup (82.5g) brown sugar**
**1½ teaspoons (3.75g) cornstarch**
**1 teaspoon (2.6g) cinnamon**
**2 cups (280g) whole milk**

In the bowl of a stand mixer, beat the apple butter, eggs, and brown sugar. Whisk together the cornstarch and cinnamon and add to the mixture. Then, add the milk and beat slowly until everything is incorporated. Pour into a par-baked or unbaked 9-inch (23cm) pie shell. Bake at 425°F for 10 minutes and then reduce heat to 350°F and bake for 30 minutes until set, but still a little jiggly.

# Apple Cream Pie

*Amish Community Cookbook*

*A luscious variation of the classic apple pie, the addition of a cream sauce poured over sliced apples gives this pie its pudding-like texture. Five cups of apples will fill a deep-dish pie. If your pie pan is shallow, reduce the apples to 4 cups.*

**Two 9-inch (23cm) pie crusts, unbaked**
**5 cups (570g) thinly sliced apples**
**1 cup (200g) white sugar**
**¼ cup (30g) all-purpose flour**
**1 pinch salt**
**¾ cup (170.25g) heavy cream**
**1 teaspoon (2.8g) cinnamon mixed with 1 tablespoon (12.38g) white sugar**
**Egg wash (1 large egg yolk mixed with 2 tablespoons [11g] heavy cream)**

Line the pie pan with the bottom pie crust. Place the sliced apples in the pie crust. Whisk together the sugar, flour, and salt, then mix with the cream, stirring until incorporated. Pour this over the apples. Mix the cinnamon with 1 tablespoon sugar and sprinkle over the apple filling. Cover with a top crust, then seal and vent. Brush top crust with an egg wash. Chill in refrigerator for about 15 minutes prior to baking so the butter in the crust gets cold again. This will help produce a flakier crust. Bake at 400°F for 10 minutes, then reduce temperature to 350°F and bake for an additional 40–45 minutes.

# Buttermilk Pie

*Amish Community Cookbook*

*I like to call this the Grandma Pie. Although my Amish grandmother passed away years before I was born, I feel sure this is a pie she would have made. It has a slightly tangy flavor of buttermilk in a custard-like filling and is comforting in its simplicity.*

**One 9-inch (23cm) pie crust, unbaked**
**1 cup (198g) white sugar**
**2 tablespoons (15g) all-purpose flour**
**½ teaspoon (3g) baking soda**
**2 tablespoons (28.25g) butter, melted**
**2 large eggs**
**1 teaspoon (5g) lemon juice**
**2 cups (448g) whole fat buttermilk**

Combine the sugar, flour, and baking soda. Beat the eggs, then add the buttermilk, lemon juice, and the sugar mixture. Whisk all together until well blended, then pour into an unbaked pie crust. Bake at 425°F for 10 minutes, then reduce temperature to 350°F and bake for an additional 35 minutes.

# Lemon Sponge Pie

*Amish Community Cookbook*

*This pie has a lemony custard topped with a fluffy sponge from egg whites folded into the batter.*

**One 9-inch (23cm) deep-dish pie crust, unbaked or par-baked**
**1 cup (200g) white sugar**
**3 tablespoons (42.38g) butter, softened**
**3 tablespoons (22.5g) all-purpose flour**
**2 large egg yolks, fork-beaten (save egg whites)**
**Zest and juice of 1 lemon**
**1 pinch salt**
**1 cup (244g) whole milk**

In the bowl of a stand mixer, beat together the butter and the sugar. Add the flour, beaten eggs, the lemon zest and juice, and salt. Mix briefly, then slowly add the milk and mix until combined. In a separate bowl with clean beaters, whip the egg whites to medium peaks, then fold them gently into the lemon mixture. Pour into an unbaked or par-baked crust. On a preheated baking sheet, bake at 400°F for 15 minutes, then reduce heat to 350°F and bake for an additional 30 minutes. Pie should still be jiggly when removed from the oven.

# Custard Pie

*Michelle Gingerich, Sugarcreek, Ohio*

*The velvety texture of custard pie is achieved with the addition of evaporated milk.*

**Two 9-inch (23cm) pie crusts, unbaked**
**1¼ cups (252g) white sugar**
**2 tablespoons (15g) all-purpose flour**
**1 pinch salt**
**4 cups (1024g) evaporated milk, divided**
**3 large eggs, separated**
**1½ teaspoons (4.51g) pure vanilla extract**

Combine sugar, flour, and salt in a bowl. Set aside. Separate the egg yolks and add 1 cup (252g) of evaporated milk. Whisk together until smooth, then add to the dry ingredients and whisk again. Heat the remaining milk to steaming and add to the first mixture. Beat the egg whites to firm peaks and fold them into the custard, along with the vanilla. Pour into 2 unbaked pie crusts. Bake at 425°F on a heated baking sheet on bottom shelf of oven for 10 minutes. Reduce heat to 350°F and bake for an additional 20 minutes until done. Pie should still be a little jiggly when removed from the oven.

# Pecan Pie

*Treasured Mennonite Recipes*

*The exchange of maple syrup for the commonly used corn syrup puts a healthier twist on this classic pie and dials down the sweetness a little.*

**One 9-inch (23cm) pie crust, unbaked**
**3 large eggs**
**¾ cup (159.75g) brown sugar**
**2 tablespoons (15g) all-purpose flour**
**1¼ cups (425g) maple syrup**
**¼ cup (56.5g) melted butter**
**1 cup (109g) chopped pecans**

Beat the eggs. Mix the flour with the sugar, then add the eggs, along with the maple syrup and butter. Stir in the pecans. Pour into a 9-inch (23cm) unbaked pie crust. Decorate with whole pecans, if desired. Bake at 400°F for 10 minutes, then reduce heat to 350°F and bake for an additional 20–30 minutes. Pie should be puffed and little jiggly when you remove it from the oven.

# Peanut Butter Cream Pie

*A classic Amish pie served in many Amish restaurants. My mother would make homemade vanilla pudding to use in this recipe and it was my favorite. As a teenager, I worked in an Amish restaurant where one of my duties was to assemble our cream pies every morning. Peanut butter cream was my favorite. You could make this with instant vanilla pudding mix, but my mother's homemade pudding is so delicious in this recipe.*

One 9-inch (23cm) pre-baked pie crust
Whipped cream, for topping

**Vanilla Pudding**
4 cups (560g) whole milk, divided
2 tablespoons (28.25g) butter
¾ cup (90g) all-purpose flour
1 cup (202g) white sugar
1 cup (165g) brown sugar
1 pinch sea salt
3 large eggs
1 tablespoon (13g) pure vanilla extract

**Peanut Butter Crumbs**
½ cup (135g) peanut butter
¾ cup (82.5g) powdered sugar

1. In a medium saucepan, heat 1 cup of milk and 2 tablespoons of butter over medium heat. Meanwhile, combine sugar, flour, egg yolks, and salt in a bowl and stir to create a paste. Gradually whisk in 1 cup of milk until smooth. Whisk this mixture slowly into the warming milk on stovetop. Whisk constantly until mixture thickens and starts to boil. Allow to boil for 1 minute, stirring constantly. Remove from heat and add vanilla. Pour into a bowl and chill.

2. For the **Peanut Butter Crumbs:** In a mixing bowl, combine the powdered sugar and peanut butter with a fork until crumbly.

**Assembly:** Place two-thirds of the peanut butter crumbs into the base of the baked pie shell. Cover with the pudding mixture and then whipped cream. Garnish with the remaining peanut butter crumbs.

# Apple Pie Squares

*Laura Mast, Millersburg, Ohio*

*These apple pie squares often showed up at Gingerich family suppers when my sister-in-law brought them for dessert. The kids loved them! (The corn flakes are optional. I often make these bars without them, and they are just as good.)*

- 2½ cups (300g) all-purpose flour
- 1 teaspoon (5.68g) salt
- 1 cup (226g) shortening or butter
- 1 large egg yolk, separated
- Corn flakes (optional)
- Milk, up to ⅔ cup (162.67g)
- 6 cups apples, finely chopped or grated
- 1 cup (200g) white sugar
- 1 teaspoon (2.64g) ground cinnamon

**Glaze**

- 1 cup (113.5g) confectioners' sugar
- 2 tablespoons (30.5g) milk
- 1 teaspoon (4g) pure vanilla extract

1. In a medium bowl, whisk together the flour and salt. Then, cut in the cold butter or shortening to form crumbs. Whisk the egg yolk in a measuring cup and add enough milk to bring it to ⅔ cup. Pour this in the bowl of crumbs and stir together briefly until dough sticks together. Form into a ball, cut in half, wrap each half in plastic wrap, and refrigerate while you peel and chop the apples.

2. After the apples have been peeled and chopped, pour them into a medium-sized bowl and stir in the sugar and cinnamon. Let them rest while you roll out the dough. Roll out one-half of the dough into a rectangle, and place in a jelly roll pan. Sprinkle 2 handfuls of corn flakes over the dough. Then, pour the apple mixture over the dough. Roll out the other half of the dough into the same size as the bottom, then place over the apples. Pinch the edges together as best you can. Beat the egg white until it's foamy, and brush over the top crust. Bake at 350°F for 45 minutes. Remove from oven and drizzle with the glaze. Cool, then cut into squares and serve.

# Chocolate Pecan Pie

*A classic pecan pie gets an elevated taste of decadence with the addition of chocolate in the base of the crust.*

One 9-inch (23cm) pie crust, unbaked
6 large eggs, beaten slightly
½ cup (113g) soft butter
½ teaspoon (2.84g) salt
6 tablespoons (45g) all-purpose flour
½ cup (100g) white sugar
½ cup (106.5g) brown sugar
2 cups (624g) maple syrup
1 cup (113g) chopped pecans
1 cup (170g) semi-sweet or dark chocolate chips

In the bowl of a stand mixer, beat the eggs slightly. Add the soft butter and mix briefly. In a medium bowl, whisk together the salt, flour, and sugar and then add to the mixer. Sprinkle in the pecans and mix until well blended. In the bottom of one unbaked crust, sprinkle ½ cup chocolate chips then cover with the pecan filling. Bake at 400°F for 15 minutes, then reduce heat to 350°F, and bake an additional 20 minutes or until pie is done. Pie should be slightly puffed up and a little jiggly when you tap on the top.

PIES

# Frozen Pumpkin Pie

*Ruth Mast, Hopewell, Ohio*

*This pie was my favorite as a child, and I'm so glad my sister preserved the recipe. I love pumpkin pie and always think it should be served year-round. This pie is delicious in early fall when the days are still warm, and the nights are turning cool. Tastes like pumpkin ice cream!*

**Pie Crust**
2 cups (250g) graham cracker crumbs
5 tablespoons (70.62g) butter, melted
1 tablespoon (8g) confectioners' sugar
1 envelope (7g) Knox Gelatine®

**Pumpkin Filling**
¾ cup (183.75g) pumpkin puree
½ cup (100g) white sugar
½ teaspoon (3g) salt
½ teaspoon (1.4g) cinnamon
¼ teaspoon (0.7g) nutmeg
¼ teaspoon (0.7g) ginger
1 quart vanilla ice cream, softened (not melted completely)

1. Mix all together and press into a 9-inch (23cm) pie pan. Freeze. **Note:** You may not need all the crumbs, depending on the size and depth of your pie pan.

2. In a large bowl, mix the pumpkin, sugar, salt, and spices. Add softened ice cream and mix well. Pour quickly into the prepared pie pan, cover with plastic wrap or aluminum foil and freeze on a flat surface. Serve with whipped cream.

# Sour Cherry Hand Pies

*These hand pies are tart and sweet, and much easier to make than a cherry pie. They are great to pack in a picnic lunch.*

Two 9-inch (23cm) pie crusts, unbaked
2 cups (308g) sour cherries, pitted and drained (save juice)
½ cup (134.5g) sour cherry juice
⅓ cup (66g) white sugar
2 tablespoons (30g) lemon juice
1 pinch salt
2 tablespoons (30g) water
1 tablespoon (8g) cornstarch
½ teaspoon (2.1g) pure vanilla extract
Egg wash (1 large egg yolk mixed with 2 tablespoons [30 g] heavy cream)

1. In a medium-sized baking pot, bring the cherries, juice, sugar, lemon juice, and salt to a boil. Boil slowly for about 3-5 minutes, then make a slurry with the water and cornstarch and pour into the boiling cherries. Stir constantly. Mixture will turn from cloudy to translucent. When the mixture is shiny and bubbling again, remove from the heat and add vanilla extract. Cool to room temperature, or place in the refrigerator to chill.

2. While the cherry filling is cooling, roll out each disc of pie dough into a large circle. Cut six 5-inch smaller circles out of each large circle of dough to make 24 hand pies. (You may reroll leftover dough once and reuse. After that, discard scraps.) Place circles on a baking sheet separated by parchment and chill in the refrigerator until you are ready to assemble.

**Assembly:** Brush egg wash on the edge of each hand pie circle. Place 2 tablespoons of cherry filling in the middle of each circle. Pinch the edges together and crimp with a fork. Cut 3 small vents in the top of each hand pie. Brush the tops of the hand pies with egg wash. Chill in refrigerator for about 15 minutes prior to baking so the butter in the crust gets cold again. This will help produce a flakier crust. Bake at 375°F for 10 minutes, then rotate the trays and bake for 10 minutes more, or until golden brown. Remove from the oven and sprinkle generously with white sugar. Alternatively, you may brush the hand pies with a **Vanilla Glaze**: whisk together 2 cups confectioners' sugar (sifted) with ⅛ cup milk or lemon juice. Brush over the hand pies.

# Concord Grape Pie

*Amish Community Cookbook*

*My father tended numerous Concord grapevines on our farm and often on summer nights I would fall asleep to the scent of ripening grapes outside my bedroom window. Harvest came in August, which meant we would make gallons and gallons of grape juice to preserve for the cold winter months ahead. There was nothing quite like a glass of grape juice and a bowl of popcorn on a Sunday night. This pie embodies the taste of those memories for me.*

**One 9-inch (23cm) pie crust, unbaked**

**Concord Grape Filling**

**5 cups (755g) Concord grapes, removed from their stems**
**1 large egg**
**1 cup (100g) white sugar**
**2 tablespoons (15g) flour**
**1 tablespoon (14.13g) butter**
**1 tablespoon (15g) lemon juice**

**Crumbs**

**½ cup (60g) all-purpose flour**
**½ cup (50g) white sugar**
**4 tablespoons (57.2g) butter, softened**

Wash the grapes and squeeze the pulp from the skins. Cook the pulp for 5 minutes and press through a sieve to separate the seeds. Beat the egg. Add sugar, flour, butter, and lemon juice. Add the skins and the pulp. Pour into an unbaked pie crust and top with crumbs made by combining the listed ingredients. Bake at 425°F for 15 minutes, then reduce heat to 375°F and bake for an additional 40 minutes until bubbly.

# A Culture of Hospitality

One of the things I've told people about being raised in a Mennonite home is that I learned how to cook for 30 at a moment's notice. While this may be a slight exaggeration, it is not far from the truth. The Amish and Mennonite culture is one built around hospitality and frequent (often unannounced) visits to each other's homes. Uncle John and his family coming to dinner? No problem, there's canned beef in the cellar to be fried and turned into browned butter gravy. There are potatoes in the pantry to be peeled, cooked and mashed. There is a garden where the fixings for a salad are within easy reach. And for dessert, there was usually an extra pastry crust in the freezer which could be made into a fresh pie.

Making things ahead of time and in large quantities was essential, whether canning and preserving garden produce for winter months, making extra loaves of bread on baking day or preparing ready-to-bake pie crusts and storing them in the freezer for last-minute company. The women in my family took pride in their hospitality and in the flavorful meals they served at the table. The food was simple and well-seasoned, the servings generous.

I remember the anticipation I felt as a child when I rode along with my parents to Sunday dinner at Harry Ella's house. (Mennonite and Amish women are often identified by the name of their husband preceding theirs.) On the way I would try to imagine what she might be cooking. Would it be her meatloaf with the ketchup and brown sugar glaze? Or would it be Yumesetti, the cheesy noodle casserole every Mennonite kid craved? For sure, there would be several kinds of pie. And then the variety of small plates my mother anticipated such as pickled red beets, bread and butter pickles, and deviled eggs. And always canned or frozen applesauce either pink or golden, depending on which varietal of apples were used to make the sauce. Even now, my taste buds come alive at the thought of these foods so essential to every Sunday dinner for as long as I can remember.

Here is a recipe for one of my mother's pies (page 43), though in the top right corner, she has written "Mose Betty", a reminder of the friend who shared it with her. This pie made its appearance each spring when rhubarb season came around. It showed up on our dinner table, at quilting bees and potlucks or neighborhood gatherings. It holds a special place in my memory, right alongside Harry Ella's Sunday meatloaf.

# Rhubarb Crumb Pie

*Rhubarb was one of my mother's favorite pies, and in this recipe the rhubarb is paired with the sweet taste of strawberries to balance the tartness.*

One 9-inch (23cm) pie crust, unbaked
2 cups (240g) fresh rhubarb, cut into chunks
1 cup (150g) fresh strawberries, cut into thick slices
1 large egg, fork-beaten
2 tablespoons (15g) all-purpose flour
1 cup (202g) white sugar
1 teaspoon (4.34g) pure vanilla extract

**Crumbs**

¾ cup (90g) all-purpose flour
⅓ cup (75.33g) salted butter, melted
½ cup (106.5g) brown sugar

Pour the rhubarb and strawberries into the pie crust. In a small bowl, combine the beaten egg, 2 tablespoons flour, 1 cup of white sugar, and vanilla. This will form a pourable paste. Pour this over the fruit in the crust. Mix crumbs in a separate bowl and pour over top of the pie. Bake at 350°F for about 50 minutes, until filling is bubbling around the edge of the pie. Cool completely before serving.

# CHAPTER 2

Growing up as a child, my life was richly storied in the adventures of fields and forest, hills and hollows of our 50-acre farm. I spent endless hours riding along on the wagon as my father hand-harvested fields of corn to be ground into feed for the animals. I climbed trees, played in the old chicken house, mucked out stalls, and helped milk our herd of dairy cows. When I was finally old enough to drive the tractor, I was permitted that fun task during hay baling season. And, as a 12-year-old, I looked for plenty of other reasons to use the tractor and experience the thrill of operating the clutch and the gear shift simultaneously.

I spent much of my time outdoors, preferring gardening and farming over housework, but a sure way to get me indoors was the prospect of baking. When mother gave me the first lesson in baking cakes, I was convinced this was the thing for me. We started out with cake mixes. It was the seventies, after all, and the invention of boxed cake mixes and Betty Crocker® 20 years prior had caused dust to gather on recipe files in kitchens, at least in ours.

The cake that stole my heart was cherry chip, with creamy white frosting out of a can. Every trip to the grocery store, that cake mix went into the cart. Years later, I still get nostalgic when I think of that cake, and I even recreated it at our bakery several years ago. (It was good, but don't judge me, the boxed cake was better.) When I finally started making cakes from scratch, I landed on chocolate cake and haven't been swayed since.

The chocolate cake I was most fond of was like the Wacky Cake recipe in this book (page 59), where the dry ingredients are mixed in the pan, three holes made, liquid ingredients poured into the holes, and everything is stirred together. I also learned how to bake Amish Neighbor Cake (page 68) and a simple Vanilla Cake (page 64) with vanilla frosting, which was my father's favorite. These were all sheet cakes. It wasn't until years later when I got out the old recipe file and blew off the dust, that I discovered a whole other world of cakes.

Most notable to me in that box of handwritten recipes were Aunt Edna's layer cakes and my mother's chiffon cakes. But in typical fashion of the 1940s and 50s, the ingredients were vaguely listed in no particular order, with penciled in phrases such as, "Add enough flour until the batter looks right," or, "Bake as usual," or, my favorite, no instructions at all. Those recipes provided inspiration for me, though, and through trial and error I was able to interpret many of them for modern day use.

When I started the bakery with my daughter, towering layer cakes became one of our specialties. I found satisfaction in working with luscious buttercreams and scratch-made fillings using seasonal local fruit to create bursts of flavor. Cakes became my artist's palette as I decorated them in free-form swirls of frosting and an array of fresh flowers and fruit.

I have included recipes in Chapter 7 (page 176) for some of the fillings I often use in cakes; however, feel free to get creative with your own, whether it's pudding, pie filling, or preserves. These fillings will take a cake from ordinary to extraordinary and will impress your guests when served for a birthday, dinner party, or holiday gathering.

## • RECIPES •

# Cakes

# How to Bake and Assemble a Layer Cake

CAKES

## Step #1: Baking a Layer Cake

**1.** One of the most important aspects of baking a layer cake is the proper preparation of your cake pans. Nothing is more disheartening than trying to remove a cake from the pan and part of it remains stuck to the bottom. I generally use 6- or 8-inch round cake pans and grease the bottom and sides with a light coat of melted butter. Then, I cover the bottom with a circle of parchment. If you don't have precut circles of parchment, you can turn your cake pans upside down and trace them on a piece of parchment, cutting it to the size of your pan. Next, I grease the parchment circle, sprinkle it with flour, and shake it all around the pan, dumping the excess. Then, I fill each pan with batter, using 1 cup per 6-inch pan, or 2 cups per 8-inch pan, or you can divide your batter evenly between pans.

**2.** After the cakes are done baking, I let them rest in their pans for about 10 minutes before inverting them onto cooling racks to cool completely. Lastly, I wrap each layer in plastic wrap (not too tight, but enough so it will be airtight) and store them on the counter overnight. While you can bake your cake the same day you assemble it, I like to bake it the day before, so the crumb has a chance to settle. This makes it easier to frost.

## Step # 2: How to Assemble a Layer Cake

**1.** Gather the tools you will need and lay them out on the surface where you will be frosting your cake. These should include a round cake turntable, a grease-resistant cardboard cake circle about 1 or 2 inches wider than your cake, an offset frosting spatula, the bowl of frosting, and your cakes. If you do not have a turn table, carefully rotate the cake by hand on a table.

**2.** Place one layer of the cake onto the cake circle. If the cake needs to be leveled, do so with a long serrated-edge knife. With a spatula, scoop out a portion of frosting and place it onto the middle of your cake. You can measure the amount of frosting, if this is helpful for you. Start with approximately 1 cup.

**3.** Next, with one hand, begin swirling and smoothing the frosting to the edge of the cake while the other hand is slowly rotating the cake turntable. Smooth it evenly across the surface of the cake, piling up more frosting around the edges. This will create a nest where you can place some filling such as preserves or lemon curd, if desired.

**4.** If you are using a filling, spoon it into the center, spreading it around within the nest, but not outside the ridges you have built around the edge.

**5.** Now you are ready to add the second layer. Place the cake evenly on top of the first layer, then scoop out another cup of frosting and repeat the process. Rotate the turntable as you smooth the frosting to the edge of the cake, all the way around, leaving a higher ridge around the outside of the cake. If you are using a filling, add a few more spoonfuls to the nest and then nestle the third layer on top.

**6.** At this point, get down to eye level with the cake, slowly rotating it to make sure all the sides are even. Then, smooth the excess frosting between the layers, creating a bit of a seal to keep them in place.

**7.** Now you are ready to add the crumb coat. Starting on the side, begin to smooth a light coat of frosting all around the cake, rotating the turntable as you go. Lastly, smooth it over the top. The goal is not to fully frost the cake at this point. You are only adding a thin layer of frosting to hold the cake together and to provide a good base to finish with a final coat. When every cake surface has been covered, place your cake on a flat surface in the refrigerator or a freezer and allow the frosting to set for about 5–10 minutes.

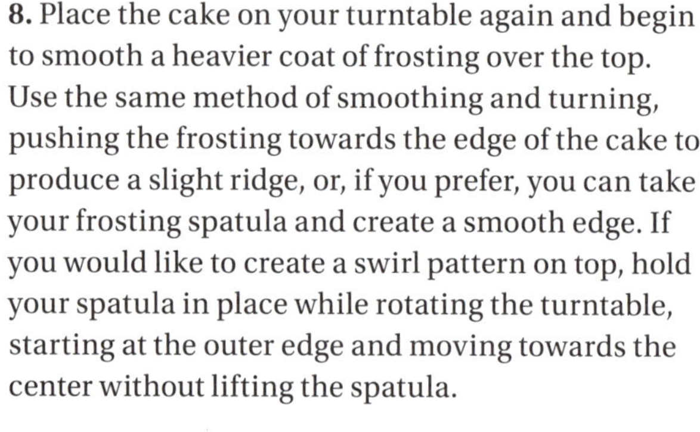

**8.** Place the cake on your turntable again and begin to smooth a heavier coat of frosting over the top. Use the same method of smoothing and turning, pushing the frosting towards the edge of the cake to produce a slight ridge, or, if you prefer, you can take your frosting spatula and create a smooth edge. If you would like to create a swirl pattern on top, hold your spatula in place while rotating the turntable, starting at the outer edge and moving towards the center without lifting the spatula.

**9.** Starting on the side, begin to smooth a heavier coat of frosting on the cake as you rotate the turntable. Continue to frost and smooth the sides until you have an even amount of frosting from top to bottom. Give the cake one final smoothing with the frosting spatula along the sides as you rotate the turntable.

*Baking and assembling a layer cake is a labor of love, and practice does make better, if not perfect. And what a beautiful gift to offer guests as they gather around your table, eagerly awaiting slices of a delicious cake you have made from start to finish!*

**10.** Now comes the fun part—decorating the cake! Your cake is a blank canvas for creativity, and this is where you can express yourself. While you are certainly welcome to decorate your cake with fancy frosting techniques, I prefer to use fresh flowers or seasonal fruit for my garnish. At the bakery, we have local flower and fruit farmers who drop off weekly deliveries for us to use for our cakes. If I am at home, I like to wander through my garden in search of tiny blossoms. Not all flowers are edible, so I always recommend people don't eat them. However, rose petals, pansies, nasturtiums, violets, lilac blossoms, and many other varieties are beautiful and safe to eat if they have not been exposed to chemical pesticides.

# Sunshine Chiffon Cake

*My mother's recipe from the 1960s for this chiffon cake is airy and moist. I love to serve it with lemon curd or fresh fruit. It is a bit denser than an angel food cake because it contains both the yolks and the whites of eggs in addition to oil.*

**1¾ cups plus 2 tablespoons (225g) all-purpose flour**
**1½ cups (303g) white sugar**
**1 tablespoon (15g) baking powder**
**1 teaspoon (5.68g) sea salt**
**½ cup (108.60g) sunflower oil**
**5 egg yolks, fork-beaten (save egg whites)**
**¾ cup (176.49g) water**
**2 teaspoons (10g) vanilla**
**7 egg whites**
**½ teaspoon (3.38g) cream of tartar**

1. In the bowl of a stand mixer, combine the flour, sugar, baking powder, and salt. Then, add the oil, egg yolks, water, and vanilla and beat for 2 minutes. Set aside.

2. In a separate bowl, beat the egg whites until foamy, then add the cream of tartar and beat until stiff peaks form. With a large wooden spoon or spatula, gently fold the stiff egg whites into the first mixture until they are incorporated. Pour into a large tube pan. (Do not grease sides.)

3. Bake at 325°F for 55 minutes, then at 350°F for 10 minutes or until a toothpick inserted comes out with some crumbs attached. Invert to cool for at least 1 hour.

4. To serve, cut the cake into slices and top with Lemon Curd (page 182) and a dollop of whipped cream, or fresh fruit.

**Note:** This is a large cake and will bake high like an angel food cake.

# Aunt Edna's Whipped Cream Cake

*This recipe from the sixties bakes up as a small two-layer, 8-inch cake perfectly suited for my mother's vintage 8-inch Ovenex® cake pans. It could also be baked as a single-layer cake in a modern 8-inch round cake pan and topped with strawberries and whipped cream. The baking time will lengthen if you bake it in one pan instead of two.*

**1½ cups (180g) cake flour***
**2 teaspoons (10g) baking powder**
**1 pinch sea salt**
**1 cup (240g) heavy cream**
**1 cup (202g) white sugar**
**2 large eggs**
**1 teaspoon (5g) pure vanilla extract**
**Whipped cream**
**Strawberries**

**If you don't have cake flour, you can use 2 tablespoons of cornstarch per cup of flour. To measure this accurately, measure out 1 cup of flour, remove 2 tablespoons, then add 2 tablespoons of cornstarch.*

In a small bowl, whisk together the flour, baking powder, and salt. In the bowl of a stand mixer, whip the cream with the sugar until stiff peaks form. Then, beat in the eggs, one at a time, and add the vanilla. Scrape the bowl, then fold in the flour mixture slowly just until incorporated. Pour batter into either one or two 8-inch greased and floured cake pans. Bake at 350°F for about 16–20 minutes until a toothpick inserted in center comes out with only a few crumbs attached. After cake has cooled completely, either assemble as a two-layer cake with whipped cream and thinly sliced strawberries between the layers, or as a single-layer cake topped with strawberries and whipped cream, like a shortcake. Serves 8–10.

# Butter Cake

*This simple cake is baked in a loaf pan and covered in a maple glaze when it comes out of the oven. It's delicious to eat plain, or to serve with a dollop of whipped cream and some fresh fruit.*

1 cup (226g) unsalted butter
1½ cups (303g) white sugar
4 large eggs
1 teaspoon (5g) pure vanilla extract
2 cups (240g) all-purpose flour
1 teaspoon (5g) baking powder
¼ teaspoon (1.42g) salt
½ cup (112g) whole-fat buttermilk

**Maple Glaze**
1 cup (202g) white sugar
1 stick (113g) of unsalted butter
2 tablespoons (40g) maple syrup
2 tablespoons (29.57g) water
1 pinch salt

1. Cream the butter and sugar together until fluffy, about 5 minutes, scraping the bowl occasionally. Add the eggs, one at a time, beating after each addition. Add the vanilla. In a medium bowl, whisk together the flour, baking powder, and salt, and then add to the first mixture alternately with the buttermilk. Mix just until the flour is incorporated. Do not overmix. Pour batter into a buttered 9 x 5-inch loaf pan that has been lined with parchment paper. Bake at 325°F for about 45 minutes, until a toothpick inserted in the center comes out with just a few crumbs attached.

2. For the **Maple Glaze**, place all ingredients into a small saucepan and bring mixture to a boil, stirring occasionally. When the edges start bubbling, remove from the heat. Brush glaze over hot loaf. It's okay to give it several coats. The glaze will harden a bit as it cools, giving the loaf a sugary crust.

# Fresh Strawberry Cake

*Clara Gingerich Miller, Dover, Delaware*

*This easy and delicious recipe speeds up the preparation process by using a cake mix and adding additional ingredients. The strawberry flavor comes through strongly with the fresh berries and the color is a vibrant pink thanks to the Jell-O.*

1 box (432g) white cake mix
4 large eggs
1 cup (217.19g) oil
½ cup (70g) milk
1 cup (65g) unsweetened shredded coconut
1 cup (167g) chopped strawberries
1 cup (113g) nuts (optional)
One 3-ounce box (85g) Strawberry Jell-O

***Fresh Strawberry Frosting: Page 182***

1. In the bowl of a stand mixer, blend the cake mix with the eggs, oil, and milk. Add the coconut, nuts (if using), and strawberries. Lastly, add the Jell-O and mix until blended. Pour the batter into a buttered and floured 9 x 13-inch cake pan and bake at 325°F for about 20 minutes or until a toothpick inserted comes out with only a few crumbs attached. Cool completely.

2. For the **Fresh Strawberry Frosting**, see page 182. Spread over cooled cake.

# Mayonnaise Cake

*This is one of the first cakes I remember baking in the seventies. Now it's interesting to see it making a comeback as bakers search through family recipes to find forgotten treasures. Don't be put off by the mayonnaise. It adds moisture and fat, and you won't be able to taste it.*

2 cups (240g) all-purpose flour
1 cup (200g) white sugar
⅓ cup (28.33g) cocoa powder
2 teaspoons (12g) baking soda
1 cup (226g) mayonnaise, room temperature
1 cup (236.59g) warm water
1 pinch salt
1 teaspoon (5g) vanilla

***Chocolate Sour Cream Frosting: Page 183***

1. In a medium-sized bowl, whisk together the flour, sugar, cocoa powder, and baking soda. In another bowl, whisk together the mayonnaise, warm water, and salt. Combine dry ingredients with the wet ingredients, add the vanilla, and stir together until well blended. Pour into a 9 x 9-inch pan and bake at 350°F for about 30 minutes until a toothpick inserted in center comes out clean.

2. For the **Chocolate Sour Cream Frosting**, see page 183.

# Flourless Chocolate Torte (gluten-free)

*I discovered the delicious taste of flourless chocolate cakes in 2014 while I was writing a food blog. The taste is rich and decadent, but the texture is also light and airy. The Raspberry Whipped Cream is delightful, but you could also garnish it with Maldon flake salt, which is how we serve it at our bakery.*

**1 cup (170g) dark chocolate chips**
**¾ cup (169.5g) unsalted butter**
**½ cup (99g) white sugar**
**¼ cup (53.25g) brown sugar**
**1 pinch salt**
**5 large eggs, separated (save whites)**
**1 teaspoon (4.3g) pure vanilla extract**

1. Put the chocolate, butter, brown sugar, and salt into a heat-proof bowl set over a pan of simmering water. (Bottom of bowl should not touch water.) Stir the mixture occasionally until it is melted together and smooth. Remove the bowl and set on a towel on countertop (to prevent sliding). Meanwhile, in the bowl of a stand mixer, beat the egg yolks with the white sugar until pale and fluffy. Then, whisk into the chocolate mixture.

2. Wash and dry the mixer bowl, then beat the egg whites until they are foamy and have soft peaks. Fold the egg whites into the chocolate mixture, along with the vanilla extract. Do not stir, but fold gently with a spatula, as we are relying on the egg whites to provide lift for the cake. When it is fully incorporated, pour into an 8-inch round cake pan that has been lined with parchment paper. Bake at 350°F for about 30 minutes. The torte should still have a slight jiggle when you remove it from the oven. It will deflate slightly as it cools. Cool completely, then transfer to a serving plate. Garnish with confectioners' sugar and serve with Raspberry Whipped Cream or flake salt.

## Raspberry Whipped Cream

**1¼ cups (283.75g) heavy cream**
**3 tablespoons (23.43g) confectioners' sugar**
**1 cup (120g) of raspberries, crushed**

Whip the cream to medium soft peaks, add the confectioners' sugar and the crushed berries, and beat again to incorporate. This cream is best when it's not beaten stiff but will drop from a spoon in a soft puddle.

# Moist Chocolate Cake

*Geneva Schlabach, Sarasota, Florida*

*This chocolate cake lives up to its name. The addition of brewed coffee in the batter enhances the flavor of the chocolate, and when topped with a creamy chocolate buttercream or a Chocolate Sour Cream Frosting (page 183), it is unbeatable. If you have gluten sensitivity, this recipe can be made using a 1:1 ratio of gluten-free flour. I tested it with Whole Cell Crushed Wheat Flour and it turned out beautifully.*

**2 cups (240g) all-purpose flour**
**2 cups (400g) white sugar**
**¾ cup (63.5g) cocoa powder**
**2 teaspoons (12g) baking soda**
**1 teaspoon (4g) baking powder**
**1 pinch salt**
**½ cup (108.59g) oil**
**1 cup (236.59g) hot coffee**
**1 cup milk, (244g) room temperature**
**2 large eggs, room temperature**

In a medium-sized bowl, whisk together the dry ingredients. In the bowl of a stand mixer, blend the oil, coffee, milk, and eggs. Add the dry ingredients and mix until incorporated. Pour batter into a greased and floured 10-inch springform pan and bake for about 50–55 minutes at 350°F. You can also pour this into a buttered and floured 9 x 13-inch cake pan and bake it for about 20 minutes or until a toothpick inserted in the center comes out with only a few crumbs attached. Frost with chocolate buttercream or Chocolate Sour Cream Frosting (page 183). (Photo shows Chocolate Sour Cream Frosting.).

# Raw Apple Cake

*Treasured Amish and Mennonite Recipes*

*Loaded with fresh apples and topped with a caramel glaze, this cake bakes up with a tender crumb.*

- 3 large eggs
- 2 cups (400g) white sugar
- 1½ cups (324g) oil
- 3 cups (360g) all-purpose flour
- 1 teaspoon (4.8g) baking soda
- 1 teaspoon (6g) salt
- 2 teaspoons (8.4g) pure vanilla extract
- 3 cups (375g) chopped apples
- 1½ cups (210g) chopped nuts, optional

**Brown Sugar Topping**

- 1 cup (225g) brown sugar
- ¼ cup (62g) milk
- ½ cup (115g) butter

Mix the eggs, sugar, and oil. Combine flour, baking soda, and salt and stir into the wet ingredients. Add the vanilla extract, apples, and nuts and stir again until combined. Pour into a buttered 9 x 13-inch baking dish. Bake at 325°F for 1 hour and 15 minutes. Baking times may vary, so keep an eye on it. Combine topping ingredients while cake is baking and boil for 2.5–3 minutes. While cake is still warm, make holes with fork tines and pour topping over the top.

# Spiced Crumb Cake

*Grandma Linda Gingerich, Millersburg, Ohio*

*This is my mother-in-law's recipe from the sixties and has been a family favorite for many years. The texture is incredibly moist from the buttermilk and the spiced crumbs on top make it a perfect cake for fall or winter.*

- 4 cups (480g) all-purpose flour
- 1 cup (226g) butter, softened
- 2 cups (396g) white sugar
- 2 teaspoons (12g) baking soda
- 1 pinch salt
- ¼ teaspoon (.7g) ginger
- ½ teaspoon (1.4g) cinnamon
- 1 teaspoon (2.8g) allspice
- ½ teaspoon (1.4g) cloves
- 2 cups (448g) buttermilk

Whisk dry ingredients together, then with a fork or your hands, blend in the butter until it resembles crumbs. Take out 1 cup of crumbs and reserve for the top. Stir 2 cups of buttermilk into the first set of crumbs and pour into a 9 x 13-inch pan. Top with the reserved crumbs. Bake at 350°F for about 22 minutes, or until a toothpick inserted in center comes out with only a few crumbs attached.

# Banana Cake

*Amish Community Cookbook*

*This cake is packed with banana flavor but is not as dense as banana bread because of the cake flour in the recipe. Soft and comforting, this cake reminds me of home.*

- ⅔ cup (138g) oil
- 2½ (300g) cups cake flour*
- 1⅔ cups (330g) white sugar
- 1¼ teaspoons (6g) baking powder
- 1 teaspoon (6g) baking soda
- 1 teaspoon (5.84g) sea salt
- 1¼ cups (256.25g) mashed bananas (about 4 medium bananas)
- ⅓ cup (74.67g) whole-fat buttermilk
- 2 large eggs

**Glaze**

- 2 cups (224g) confectioners' sugar, sifted
- 4 tablespoons (60.92g) milk
- 2 teaspoons (14g) pure vanilla extract

**I rarely have cake flour in my pantry, so for recipes that call for it, I use the equivalent of 2 tablespoons of cornstarch per cup of all-purpose flour. I do this by measuring 2 tablespoons of cornstarch into a cup and then filling it up the rest of the way with all-purpose flour.*

Measure oil into the bowl of a stand mixer. Sift flour, sugar, baking powder, baking soda, and salt together and add to the bowl. With the mixer on low speed, begin to blend and then add the eggs, one at a time, and then the mashed bananas and the buttermilk. Increase the speed to medium and blend for about 30 seconds. Pour batter into a buttered and floured angel food cake pan or bundt pan and bake at 325°F for about 35 minutes, or until a toothpick inserted in center comes out with only a few crumbs attached. Allow to cool for about 10 minutes, then remove from pan and transfer to a wire rack to cool completely. Whisk together the ingredients for the Glaze, then drizzle over cake.

# Mattie's Cake

*Ruth Mast, Hopewell, Ohio*

*This recipe is from my sister, and it is a truly moist and decadent chocolate cake. It can be baked in two 8-inch round cake pans or in an angel food cake pan. I used an angel food cake pan and frosted only the top with cream cheese frosting.*

**7 tablespoons (37.19g) cocoa powder**
**2 cups (400g) white sugar**
**3 cups (360g) all-purpose flour**
**2 teaspoons (12g) baking soda**
**1 teaspoon (5.68g) salt**
**1 cup (217.18g) oil**
**2 cups (473.18g) cold water**
**2 tablespoons (28.7g) vinegar**
**2 tablespoons (26g) vanilla**

In the bowl of a stand mixer, add all the ingredients and mix until blended. Then, pour into 2 buttered and floured 8-inch round cake pans or into one angel food cake pan and bake at 350°F. For the round pans, bake approximately 20 minutes, and the angel food cake pan for about 40 minutes or until a toothpick inserted in center comes out with only a few crumbs attached. Cool, then frost with your favorite icing.

# Wacky Cake

*Amish Community Cookbook*

*This is one of the first cakes I started baking around age 13. I used to call it Crazy Cake. It's easy, mixes in the pan you bake it in (which means less dishes to wash), and it turns out well every single time. Win, win, win.*

**3 cups (360g) all-purpose flour**
**2 cups (400g) white sugar**
**½ cup (42.5g) cocoa powder**
**2 teaspoons (12g) baking soda**
**1 teaspoon (5.84g) sea salt**
**2 tablespoons (30g) vinegar**
**2 teaspoons (14g) pure vanilla extract**
**⅔ cup (137.06g) oil**
**2 cups (473.18g) water**

Sift the first 5 ingredients into an ungreased 9 x 12-inch cake pan. Mix with a whisk, then make 3 holes. Pour vinegar, vanilla, and oil into the holes. Pour water over everything and mix with a whisk or wooden spoon until all ingredients are blended. Bake at 350°F for 20 minutes until a toothpick inserted in the center comes out with only a few crumbs attached. When cool, frost with your favorite frosting. (My favorite is Salted Caramel Buttercream on page 181.)

CAKES

# Upside-Down Cake

*A simply written recipe from the fifties by Aunt Edna, this is a versatile cake to make with whatever fruit you have in the refrigerator. Often it was made with pineapple rings and maraschino cherries, but it can be made with any kind of berry or stone fruit (I used cranberries for this recipe). The fruit is placed on the bottom of the pan with the cake batter scooped over the top, then it is inverted onto a cake plate immediately upon removal from the oven.*

**4 large egg yolks**
**1½ cups (300g) white sugar, divided**
**3 tablespoons (44.36g) hot water**
**1 cup (120g) all-purpose flour**
**1 teaspoon (5g) baking powder**
**1 pinch salt**
**1 teaspoon (4.3g) pure vanilla extract**
**4 large egg whites**
**3–4 tablespoons (42.5g–56.7g) butter, melted**
**2 cups (198g) cranberries or any berry or stone fruit (grams will vary depending on fruit)**

1. In the bowl of a stand mixer, combine the egg yolks and sugar and whip until blended. Whisk the flour, baking powder, and salt together, then add those to the mixer along with the hot water and vanilla extract. Beat until blended. The batter will be thick. Scrape into a mixing bowl and set aside. Whip the egg whites until they form soft peaks (not too hard or it will be difficult to mix into the batter). With a spatula, fold the egg whites into the batter. Be patient and keep folding until it's all incorporated.

2. Prepare a 9- or 10-inch round cake pan by pouring 3–4 tablespoons of melted butter into the pan and spreading all around. Pour the fruit on top of the batter. If you have slices of peaches or plums, you can arrange them artistically, snuggling them in single layer close together (at least 2 cups). I used cranberries in this recipe, so I just spread them around the bottom of the pan evenly. Next, sprinkle ½ cup sugar over the fruit, then top with dollops of the batter, spreading all around to the edges. Bake at 350°F for about 25–30 minutes until a toothpick inserted comes out with only a few crumbs attached.

3. Remove from the oven and within 5 minutes, invert onto a cake plate. Hint: Take a sharp knife, loosen the cake all around the edges, then, wearing oven mitts, rest the cake plate upside down directly onto the baking pan, grab both the baking pan and the plate, and turn them over quickly, setting the plate on the counter. Remove the baking pan. It feels like a tricky process, but it works. **Just don't let the cake cool in the pan or it will become sticky and impossible to invert.** To serve, cut into slices and top with dollops of sweetened whipped cream.

# Peanut Butter Banana Cake

*For a different take on the Banana Cake recipe by Amish Community Cookbook (page 58), bake this cake in a 10 x 10-inch pan and cover it in swirls of Peanut Butter Frosting (page 181). Cut into fat squares and serve with a cup of coffee or glass of milk.*

**⅔ cup (138g) oil**
**2½ (300g) cups *cake flour**
**1 cup (213g) brown sugar**
**⅔ cup (132g) white sugar**
**1¼ teaspoons (6g) baking powder**
**1 teaspoon (6g) baking soda**
**1 teaspoon (5.84g) sea salt**
**1¼ cups (256.25g) mashed bananas (about 4 medium bananas)**
**⅓ cup (74.67g) whole-fat buttermilk**
**2 large eggs**

***Peanut Butter Frosting: Page 181***

**I rarely have cake flour in my pantry, so for recipes that call for it, I use the equivalent of 2 tablespoons of cornstarch per cup of all-purpose flour. I do this by measuring 2 tablespoons of cornstarch into a cup and then filling it up the rest of the way with all-purpose flour.*

1. Measure oil into the bowl of a stand mixer. Sift flour, sugar, baking powder, baking soda, and salt together and add to the bowl. With the mixer on low speed, begin to blend and then add the eggs, one at a time, and then the mashed bananas and the buttermilk. Increase the speed to medium and blend for about 30 seconds. Pour batter into a buttered and floured 10 x 10-inch cake pan and bake at 325°F for about 30 minutes, or until a toothpick inserted in center comes out with only a few crumbs attached. Allow to cool completely, then frost with Peanut Butter Frosting.

2. For the **Peanut Butter Frosting**, see page 181.

# Pumpkin Cake

*Warm spices compliment the taste of pumpkin in this moist sheet cake. Covered in Cream Cheese Frosting, it is a delicious dessert to serve in fall.*

1 cup (213g) brown sugar
1 cup (200g) white sugar
2 cups (240g) all-purpose flour
¾ teaspoon (4.28g) sea salt
2 teaspoons (5.6g) ground cinnamon
2 teaspoons (5.6g) ground ginger
1 teaspoon (2.8g) ground cloves
2 teaspoons (9.6g) baking powder
2 teaspoons (11.38g) baking soda
1 cup (210g) olive oil
4 large eggs, room temperature
One 15-ounce can (425.24g) pumpkin puree

**Cream Cheese Frosting**

1 cup (226g) unsalted butter, softened
4 ounces (113.4g) cream cheese, softened
2 cups (224g) confectioners' sugar
½ teaspoon (3g) sea salt
1 teaspoon (4.2g) pure vanilla extract

1. In a medium-sized mixing bowl, whisk together the sugar, flour, spices, baking powder, and baking soda. In the bowl of a stand mixer, beat the oil, eggs, and pumpkin until blended, then add the dry ingredients. Beat until well blended. Pour into a buttered 9 x 13-inch baking pan. Bake at 325°F for about 25 minutes, or until a toothpick inserted in center comes out with only a few crumbs attached. When cool, cover with Cream Cheese Frosting.

2. For the **Cream Cheese Frosting**, whip butter and cream cheese on medium-high speed until light and creamy, about 4 minutes. Reduce speed and gradually add confectioners' sugar, sea salt, and vanilla. Then, increase speed and beat for a few more minutes until fluffy.

# Spice Cake

*Grandma Linda Gingerich, Millersburg, Ohio*

*Warm spices and the tang of buttermilk combine to give this cake its comforting taste, especially when covered in Cream Cheese Frosting (page 65).*

- 1 cup (226g) shortening or butter
- 2 cups (400g) white sugar
- 2 large eggs, room temperature
- 4 cups (480g) all-purpose flour
- 2 teaspoons (10g) baking soda
- 1 teaspoon (5g) baking powder
- ½ teaspoon (2.84g) sea salt
- 2 teaspoons (5.6g) ground cinnamon
- ½ teaspoon (1.4g) ground cloves
- ½ teaspoon (1.4g) ground allspice
- 2 cups (448g) buttermilk, room temperature
- 4 tablespoons (60g) Karo or maple syrup

In the bowl of a stand mixer, beat the butter and the sugar together until creamy, about 4 minutes. In a medium mixing bowl, whisk together the flour, baking soda, baking powder, spices, and salt. To the butter and sugar mixture, add the eggs, one at a time, and mix again until incorporated. Next add the dry ingredients alternately with the buttermilk, scraping the bowl. Lastly, add the Karo or maple syrup and mix until blended. Pour into a 9 x 13-inch buttered cake pan and bake at 350°F for about 30 minutes or until a toothpick inserted comes out with only a few crumbs attached. When cake is cool, frost with Cream Cheese Frosting (page 65).

# Vanilla Cake

*A vanilla layer cake for birthdays or other special occasions. I like to add preserves between the layers, but you may also leave it plain. It is delicious with chocolate or vanilla buttercream.*

- 1 cup (217.19g) olive oil or sunflower oil
- ½ cup (113.5g) sour cream, room temperature
- 3 large eggs, room temperature
- 2 cups (400g) white sugar
- 1 tablespoon (15g) pure vanilla extract
- 1½ cups (336g) buttermilk
- 3¾ cups (390g) all-purpose flour, sifted
- 1 teaspoon (6g) baking soda
- 1 teaspoon (5g) baking powder
- 1 teaspoon (5.84g) sea salt

In the bowl of a stand mixer, beat the oil, sour cream, eggs, sugar, vanilla, and buttermilk. In a medium bowl, whisk together the flour, baking soda, baking powder, and sea salt. Slowly add the dry ingredients to the wet ingredients, scraping the bowl and mixing just until incorporated. Divide batter into three 8-inch cake pans lined with parchment paper. Bake at 350°F for approximately 16 minutes, or until a toothpick inserted in the center comes out with only a few crumbs attached.

# Carrot Cake

*Amish Community Cookbook*

*Packed with carrots and toasted nuts, this carrot cake is gently spiced with cinnamon and covered in a Cream Cheese Frosting.*

**4 large eggs**
**2 cups (400g) white sugar**
**1½ cups (325.79g) oil**
**1 teaspoon (7g) pure vanilla extract**
**3 cups (366g) shredded carrots**
**2 cups (240g) all-purpose flour**
**2 teaspoons (12g) baking soda**
**1 teaspoon (5g) baking powder**
**1½ teaspoons (3.9g) ground cinnamon**
**1 teaspoon (5.84g) sea salt**
**1 cup (130g) chopped walnuts or pecans, lightly toasted**

### Cream Cheese Frosting

**1 cup (226g) unsalted butter, softened**
**6 ounces (170.1g) cream cheese, room temperature**
**2 teaspoons (14g) pure vanilla extract**
**2 cups (225g) of confectioners' sugar**
**¼ teaspoon (1.42g) salt**

1. On a baking sheet, toast the chopped nuts at 350°F for about 5–8 minutes. Remove from the oven to cool. Then, in the bowl of a stand mixer, beat the eggs until light and fluffy. Add the sugar and beat for a few more minutes until creamy, then add oil, vanilla, and carrots. In a medium bowl, whisk together the flour, baking soda, baking powder, cinnamon, and salt. Add the dry ingredients to the egg/sugar mixture and stir in the nuts. Pour into an ungreased 9 x 13-inch cake pan and bake at 350°F for 30 minutes or until a toothpick inserted in the center comes out with a few crumbs attached. Cool completely, then spread with Cream Cheese Frosting.

2. For the **Cream Cheese Frosting**: in the bowl of a stand mixer, beat the butter and cream cheese until soft and fluffy, about 5–8 minutes. Add the confectioners' sugar a little at a time, then add the vanilla. Whip for at least 1 minute until it is well combined.

# Orange Layer Cake

*The recipe for this delicate orange cake was written in my mother's elegant script and buried in a recipe box for many years before I discovered it. The tender crumb and fruity aroma are complimented by a tangy Cream Cheese Frosting (page 65), although a chocolate buttercream would be good, too.*

**1½ cups (297g) white sugar**
**½ cup (113g) butter, at room temperature**
**Grated zest of 1 orange**
**2¼ cups (270g) cake flour**
**2 teaspoons (10g) baking powder**
**1 teaspoon (5.69g) salt**
**¼ teaspoon (1.25g) baking soda**
**¼ cup (62g) fresh orange juice with some pulp, room temperature**
**¾ cup (183g) whole milk, room temperature**
**2 large eggs, room temperature**

In the bowl of a stand mixer, combine the sugar and orange zest and massage together with your fingers to release the oils and aroma of the zest into the sugar. Then, add the butter and beat until well blended, scraping the bowl several times in the process. Add the eggs, one at a time, beating until incorporated after each addition. Whisk together the flour, baking powder, salt, and baking soda, and add the milk and orange juice alternately. Beat until combined, scraping the bowl. Divide batter (2 cups each) between two 8-inch round, buttered and floured cake pans, lined with a circle of parchment paper and bake at 350°F for 27–30 minutes until toothpick inserted comes out clean or with only a few crumbs attached. Allow to cool in pans for 15 minutes, then invert onto a cooling rack to cool completely before frosting with Cream Cheese Frosting (page 65).

# Chocolate Layer Cake

*Super moist and a perfect size for three 8-inch layers, this chocolate cake is a delicious choice for birthdays or special occasions. Dress it up with preserves or fruit compote in between the layers, or frost all over with your choice of frosting, and it will become a favorite.*

**1 cup (226g) butter, at room temperature**
**2 cups (396g) white sugar**
**2 large eggs, at room temperature**
**1 tablespoon (15g) vinegar**
**1 cup (244g) milk, at room temperature**
**2½ cups (280g) all-purpose flour**
**2 teaspoons (12g) baking soda**
**½ teaspoon (2.84g) salt**
**½ cup (42.5g) cocoa powder**
**1 cup (236.59g) hot water**
**1 teaspoon (4.3g) pure vanilla extract**

In the bowl of a stand mixer, blend together the butter and sugar for several minutes. Scrape the bowl, then add the eggs, one at a time, blending after each addition. Mix the vinegar and milk together and set aside. Whisk together the flour, baking soda, salt, and cocoa powder then add to the butter/sugar mixture alternately with the milk/vinegar and the hot water. Last, add the vanilla, scrape the bowl thoroughly (the butter likes to hang out in the bottom of the bowl), and blend for 1 minute until combined. Divide batter into three 8-inch cake pans (approximately 2 cups of batter per pan) that have been buttered, floured, and covered with parchment circles. Bake at 350°F for 25-30 minutes until a toothpick inserted comes out clean or with only a few crumbs attached. Cool for 15 minutes in pans before inverting onto a cooling rack to cool completely. Frost with your favorite frosting. Cake seen here is topped with Vanilla Buttercream (page 188) and Rosemary Sugared Cranberries (page 186).

# A Story About a Cake

As a child, I would sneak into the kitchen at night to eat slices of oatmeal cake when hunger pangs hit. Crossed-legged on the floor while the cicadas droned and the smell of freshly mown hay hung heavy on the night air, I cradled this cake in my hands, eating every crumb.

Years later when my mother passed away and my siblings and I were gathered under the maple tree in the front yard of the home place, an Amish neighbor came walking across the fields, a still-warm pan of oatmeal cake in his hands. We ate generous slices while we remembered our mother and the beautiful times we had growing up on the farm.

This cake is in memory of Mother and that kind neighbor who brought a taste of comfort to our family when we needed it. I call it The Amish Neighbor Cake, a humble oatmeal cake covered in a broiled Coconut Pecan Glaze.

## Amish Neighbor Cake

- 1½ cups (353g) boiling water
- 1 cup (99g) organic oats
- ½ cup (113g) unsalted butter
- 1 cup (202g) white sugar
- 1 cup (165g) brown sugar
- 1½ cups (180g) all-purpose flour
- 1 teaspoon (4g) baking powder
- ½ teaspoon (2.84g) salt
- 1 teaspoon (2.8g) cinnamon
- 2 large eggs, fork beaten
- 1 teaspoon (5g) pure vanilla extract

**Coconut Pecan Glaze**

- 1 cup (165g) brown sugar
- ½ cup (113g) butter
- ¼ cup (62g) heavy cream
- 1 cup (113g) toasted, chopped pecans
- 1 cup (65.16g) shredded unsweetened coconut

1. Place the oats and the butter into a small bowl and pour boiling water over it. Let this rest for 10 minutes while you prepare the other ingredients. In the bowl of a stand mixer, whisk the dry ingredients together, then add the beaten eggs, the oat mixture, and the vanilla. Mix until well blended, then pour into a buttered 9 x 13-inch pan. Bake at 350°F for approximately 30 minutes until a knife inserted in the center comes out with a few crumbs attached. Remove cake from the oven and increase oven temperature to broil. Then, cover cake with the Coconut Pecan Glaze and slide under the broiler for about 2–3 minutes until edges start to bubble and it is lightly browned. Watch closely!

2. For the **Coconut Pecan Glaze**: In a medium pot, heat the sugar, butter, and heavy cream for about 3 minutes until bubbling, then remove from heat and stir in the coconut and toasted pecans. Pour over hot cake and broil for 2–3 minutes (see instructions above).

# CHAPTER 3

My earliest food memory is of standing on a little stool at the stove beside my mother, helping her stir a pot of pudding. "Come help me stir the pudding," she always suggested after she had poured the thickening agent into the steaming milk, farm fresh eggs, and brown sugar. And I was happy to oblige because I knew my reward would be a warm bowl of pudding when it was done.

This pudding was something special, yet not complex. Passed down orally through many generations of our Swiss German ancestors, there was never a written recipe as my mother knew just how much of everything to add. My older siblings knew it by the German word *brei*. I simply knew it as pudding. To me, it was the only pudding that really mattered. The taste was comforting like a thin custard, not too sweet, and immensely gratifying when eaten by the spoonful from a bowl cradled in one's lap.

My children learned to love this pudding, too, and often requested it when going to Grandma's house for a meal, which was sometimes daily since we all lived on the family farm until the kids were in their early teens. And while Grandma didn't make the pudding at every request, she made it often enough for it to live in the banks of their childhood memories.

Apple dumplings were my father's most requested dessert. We lived in a county where there were abundant orchards with many varieties of apples to choose from. Often when he was out driving the country roads, he would stop by an orchard and buy a peck of his favorites: Golden Delicious, Macintosh, or Cortland. And then mother would make the dumplings for dinner, and we would eat them warm with milk, alongside a simple bowl of egg Dutch. What a treat that was!

We had a different way of making our apple dumplings. Instead of wrapping a piece of dough around a whole cored apple, mother would roll the dough out in a rectangle, like for cinnamon rolls. Then, she brushed a generous amount of butter over the dough, covered it with sliced apples, and sprinkled it with cinnamon. Next, we rolled it up like a jelly roll, sliced it, and laid it in pans to bake in a brown sugar syrup. Delicious!

Beyond the pudding and apple dumplings, there are other recipes which I always associate with our Amish and Mennonite heritage. Cherry Delight (page 80) showed up at every reunion and potluck I can remember. Date Pudding (page 83) was always served at Thanksgiving and Christmas. Fruit cobblers, Apple Crisp (page 87), graham cracker pudding, and tapioca pudding (Tapioca Fluff, page 75) all enjoyed their place at the table. Homemade ice cream was a treat we always enjoyed in the winter, often using snow to freeze it instead of ice as we turned the crank by hand. And, of course, there were always pies and cakes, but those deserve their own chapter.

In recent years, I have enjoyed making ice cream-cookie sandwiches. They represent my deep love of ice cream and cookies as a child, and when put together, they offer a fun, hand-held treat that young and old adore. They are wonderful to serve at backyard barbeques, or during a lazy Sunday on the front porch or around a campfire in the fall.

I like to think desserts are the star of the show at the dinner table. Whether fanciful or simple, eaten outside or in, they add a sense of indulgence to end a lovely meal. It's my way of saying, "I did this for you because I love you."

## • RECIPES •

# Desserts & Sweets

# How to Make Silky Chocolate Oreo® Pudding

*This silky chocolate pudding is reminiscent of French chocolate pie, but cradled in an Oreo cookie crust.*

## Ingredients

1 cup (248g) heavy whipping cream
⅔ package of Oreos from a 1 lb. 2.12 ounces (513g) package
3 tablespoons (42.38g) butter, melted
½ cup (87g) semi-sweet chocolate chips
½ cup (113g) butter
3 large eggs
¾ cup (148.5g) white sugar

***Homemade Whipped Cream: Page 184.***

**1.** Gather all your ingredients together and set them in place. Then, in the bowl of a stand mixer, whip the cream until it reaches medium peaks. Scrape into a bowl and place in refrigerator until you are ready for it.

**2.** Next, crush 2 rows of Oreo cookies and mix with 3 tablespoons melted butter. Press into the bottom of a 9 x 12-inch baking pan.

**3.** In a microwaveable container, heat the chocolate chips and butter until melted. Stir to combine until smooth and set aside.

**4.** Meanwhile, in a medium mixing bowl placed over a pot of simmering water (bottom of bowl should not touch water), whisk the eggs and the sugar together until the sugar has completely dissolved, and the eggs are pale and frothy.

**5.** Remove from the heat and cool for about 10 minutes, then whisk in the melted chocolate mixture.

**6.** Pour into the bowl of a stand mixer, and with the whisk attachment, begin to beat at high speed for about 5 minutes.

**7.** Scrape the bowl and beat again for about 4 more minutes. The mixture will have turned from dark to more of a milk chocolate mixture. Remove the mixer bowl and fold in the Homemade Whipped Cream.

**8.** Pour over the Oreo crust.

**9.** Top with additional Homemade Whipped Cream and Oreo cookie crumbs.

# Pumpkin Rollup

*Rose Gingerich*

*A favorite during fall and winter holidays, this spiced Pumpkin Rollup is easy to make and tastes delicious with its Cream Cheese Filling.*

- 1 cup (200g) white sugar
- ⅔ cup (163.33g) pumpkin puree
- 3 large eggs
- 1 teaspoon (5g) lemon juice
- 1 cup (120g) all-purpose flour
- 1 teaspoon (2.6g) ground cinnamon
- 1 teaspoon (2.6g) ginger
- ¼ teaspoon (.65g) cloves
- 1 teaspoon (6g) baking soda
- 1 pinch salt

**Cream Cheese Filling**

- 1 cup (130g) powdered sugar
- 8 ounces (226.8g) cream cheese
- 1 teaspoon (4.2g) vanilla
- 1 tablespoon (14.13g) butter

In the bowl of a stand mixer, mix the eggs, sugar, pumpkin, and lemon juice. Whisk the dry ingredients together and blend into the egg mixture. Pour into a jelly roll pan lined with parchment paper. Bake at 350°F for 15 minutes. Turn onto clean kitchen towel sprinkled generously with powdered sugar. Roll towel and cake together. Refrigerate for 10 minutes. Unroll and spread with filling. Roll up cake again and store in freezer. Prior to serving, allow to thaw and then sprinkle with powdered sugar before slicing.

# Tapioca Fluff

*Amish Community Cookbook*

*A traditional cooked tapioca pudding.*

- 3 cups (732g) whole milk
- 3 tablespoons (36g) quick-cooking tapioca
- ¾ cup (148.5g) white sugar, divided
- 2 large egg yolks, fork-stirred
- 2 large egg whites, beaten

Heat the milk, tapioca, ½ cup (99g) of white sugar, and the egg yolks in a medium saucepan. When boiling, cook and stir for 5 minutes. Remove from the heat. Meanwhile, beat the eggs whites with ¼ cup (49.5g) sugar until medium peaks form. Fold this into the tapioca mixture until thoroughly incorporated. Pour into individual serving bowls. Serves 6.

# Coconut Poke Cake

*A throwback to the poke cakes I used to make as a teenager during the seventies, this one is made from scratch. The base layer is a moist coconut cake covered in coconut milk and sweetened condensed milk, which is then covered in a silky layer of homemade Coconut Pudding and topped with Homemade Whipped Cream (page 184) and shredded coconut. Spoon it into bowls, straight from the refrigerator and watch your guests devour it!*

2¼ cups (270g) all-purpose flour
¼ cup (32g) cornstarch
2 teaspoons (10g) baking powder
½ teaspoon (2.5g) baking soda
1 teaspoon (5.69g) sea salt
¾ cup (163.49g) oil
1⅓ cup (266.67g) white sugar
3 large eggs, room temperature
¼ cup (56g) full fat buttermilk, room temperature
1 teaspoon (4.3g) pure vanilla extract
½ teaspoon (2.15g) coconut extract
⅓ cup (26.6g) shredded coconut, plus a little bit extra for sprinkling over final dessert
One 13.66-ounce (403 mL) can unsweetened coconut milk, divided

**Coconut Pudding**

2¾ cups (671g) whole milk, divided
¾ cup (151.59g) white sugar
½ teaspoon (2.84g) sea salt
3 tablespoons (21g) cornstarch
4 large egg yolks, beaten
2 tablespoons (28.25g) unsalted butter
1 teaspoon (5g) pure vanilla extract
½ teaspoon (2.5g) coconut extract

**Coconut Glaze**

The remaining coconut milk from the can, about ¾ cup
½ cup (155g) sweetened condensed milk

1. In a medium bowl, whisk the flour, cornstarch, baking powder, baking soda, and salt together. In the bowl of a stand mixer, beat the oil and the sugar for several minutes, then add the eggs, beating thoroughly to combine. Add the buttermilk, extracts, and coconut, then the dry ingredients. Mix just until combined and then stir in 1 cup (240g) of coconut milk. (Save the rest of the coconut milk in the can for the Coconut Glaze.) Pour into a large baking dish that has been buttered. I used a 9 x 14-inch rectangular pottery baking pan. Bake at 325°F for about 20–28 minutes until a toothpick inserted in the center comes out with only a few crumbs attached. Remove from the oven and set it on the counter to cool.

2. For the **Coconut Pudding**: In a medium pot, heat 2 cups of milk. Meanwhile, in a medium bowl, whisk together ½ cup (61g) milk, sugar, salt, and the beaten egg yolks. In a measuring cup, make a slurry with the cornstarch and the remaining ¼ cup (30.5g) of milk. When the milk on the stovetop is steaming, whisk in the milk/sugar/egg mixture, stirring constantly, then drizzle in the slurry of cornstarch and milk. Whisk continuously until the pudding begins to bubble, then remove from the heat and stir in the butter and extracts. Pour into a bowl to cool, covering the top with a layer of wax paper or plastic wrap placed directly on top of the pudding to prevent the forming of a hard skin. When pudding has cooled, place in refrigerator until you are ready to assemble the cake.

3. For the **Coconut Glaze**, whisk together the 2 milks. With the tines of a fork, poke holes throughout the cooled Coconut Cake, then pour the glaze over the cake. Refrigerate.

**Assembly:** Remove the cake with the glaze from the refrigerator, whisk the pudding to loosen it up, then smooth the pudding over the cake. Top with a layer of Homemade Whipped Cream (page 184) and sprinkle with shredded coconut. Refrigerate until ready to serve.

# Hot Fudge Cake

*This easy chocolate dessert is made with pantry staples and turns out great every time.*

- 1 cup (120g) all-purpose flour
- ¾ cup (148.5g) white sugar
- 3 tablespoons (15.93g) cocoa powder
- 2 teaspoons (10g) baking powder
- ¼ teaspoon (1.5g) salt
- ¾ cup (183g) milk
- ¼ cup (54.29g) oil
- 1 teaspoon (4.3g) pure vanilla extract

**Hot Fudge**

- 1 cup (213g) brown sugar, packed
- ¼ cup (31.25g) cocoa powder
- 1½ cups (354.88g) boiling water

1. In a medium-sized bowl, whisk together the dry ingredients for the cake, then whisk in the milk, oil, and vanilla. Pour into a 9 x 13-inch buttered baking pan.

2. To make the **Hot Fudge**: mix the brown sugar and cocoa powder and sprinkle it over the batter in the pan. Pour the boiling water slowly over everything. Do not stir. Bake at 350°F for approximately 25–30 minutes. A lovely cake will form on top during the baking process and underneath will be a delicious layer of hot fudge. Serve warm with ice cream.

# Vanilla Pudding

*This pudding can be used as a filling for cream pies or served in a bowl topped with whipped cream or fruit.*

- 2¾ cups (671g) whole milk, divided
- ¾ cup (151.59g) white sugar
- ½ teaspoon (2.84g) sea salt
- 3 tablespoons (21g) cornstarch
- 4 large egg yolks, beaten
- 3 tablespoons (42.38g) unsalted butter
- 2 teaspoons (10g) pure vanilla extract

1. Heat 2 cups of milk. Meanwhile in a medium bowl, whisk together ½ cup (61g) milk, sugar, salt, and beaten egg yolks. In a small bowl, make a slurry of the cornstarch and the remaining ¼ cup (30.5g) of milk. When the milk on the stovetop is almost steaming, whisk in the milk/sugar/egg mixture, stirring constantly, then drizzle in the slurry of cornstarch and milk. Whisk continuously until the pudding begins to bubble. Let it boil for close to a minute, then remove from heat and stir in the butter and vanilla. Pour into a bowl to cool, and cover with a layer of plastic wrap or wax paper directly on the pudding to keep a skin from forming while it cools.

2. If using for pie, pour into baked pie crusts when lukewarm and then chill before adding toppings. If using for pudding, refrigerate until ready to serve.

# *Brei*: A German Pudding

*Elsie Stutzman, Sugarcreek, Ohio*

*This is the pudding of my childhood. It's not too sweet, incredibly comforting, always eaten warm, and made with ingredients you likely already have in your pantry.*

**2 cups (488g) whole milk, divided**
**2½ tablespoons (18.75g) all-purpose flour**
**¼ cup (49.5g) white sugar**
**1 large egg yolk, fork beaten**
**1 pinch salt**
**1 teaspoon (4.3g) pure vanilla extract**

In a medium saucepan, heat 1¾ cups (427g) milk. Meanwhile, in a small bowl, whisk together the sugar, flour, and salt. Add the beaten egg yolk and ¼ cup (61g) milk and whisk until smooth. When the milk is bubbling around the edges, whisk in the egg mixture and continue whisking constantly until the pudding has come to a boil. Remove from the heat and stir in the vanilla. Spoon into bowls and serve warm. Sprinkle with brown sugar, if desired.

# *Opel Kuchen* (Apple Fritters)

*Treasured Amish and Mennonite Recipes*

*These little fritters have a tender and airy dough studded with apples, are not too sweet and are made from an old German recipe. You could also dip them in a donut glaze, but I think they are less sweet when sprinkled with confectioners' sugar.*

**1 large egg, beaten**
**½ cup (122g) milk**
**½ teaspoon (3.5g) baking powder**
**¼ teaspoon (1.42g) salt**
**1 cup (120g) all-purpose flour**
**Apples, cut into small chunks (approximately 2 small apples)**

Mix all ingredients except for apples. Add as many cut apples as the batter will hold. Drop by the spoonful into deep fat at 375°F. Fry on both sides. Drain on absorbent paper. Sprinkle with confectioners' sugar and eat.

# Cherry Delight

*The dessert most likely to show up at Amish and Mennonite gatherings, this Cherry Delight has been a staple around our table for many years. A graham cracker crust is topped with cream cheese whipped cream and covered in a Sour Cherry Compote (page 191) making it an easy dessert for taking away or staying home.*

**Graham Cracker Crust**
2 cups (120g) graham cracker crumbs
8 tablespoons (113g) butter, melted
3 tablespoons (37.14g) white sugar

**Cream Cheese Whipped Cream**
8 ounces (22.6g) cream cheese
1 cup (110g) confectioners' sugar, sifted
2 cups (496g) heavy whipping cream
1 teaspoon (4.2g) pure vanilla extract

***Sour Cherry Compote: Page 191***

1. **For the Graham Cracker Crust:** In a medium bowl, stir together the crumbs, butter, and sugar. Press into the bottom of a 9 x 13-inch pan and put in freezer to chill.

2. For the **Cream Cheese Whipped Cream:** In the bowl of a stand mixer, whip the cream cheese and confectioners' sugar together until well blended. Drizzle in the cream slowly until fully incorporated. Scrape the bowl and whip until it reaches a medium spreadable consistency. Stir in the vanilla. Pour over the top of the Graham Cracker Crust and refrigerate until filling is set.

3: For the **Sour Cherry Compote:** see page 191. When the cherry compote has cooled, pour over the Cream Cheese Whipped Cream and refrigerate until ready to serve.

**Note:** My mother-in-law makes this using canned cherry pie filling, and it is equally delicious.

# Bread Pudding

*Amish Community Cookbook*

*Warm and comforting, this dish can be eaten for dessert although it's equally delightful at breakfast. It reminds me of baked French toast.*

- 2 cups (488g) whole milk or half-and-half
- ¼ cup (56.5g) butter
- ⅓ cup (71g) brown sugar
- 3 large eggs
- 2 teaspoons (5.2g) ground cinnamon
- ¼ teaspoon (.65g) ground nutmeg
- 1 teaspoon (4.3g) pure vanilla extract
- 3 cups (approximately 63g) bread torn into pieces (French bread works well)

**Sauce**

- ⅓ cup (66g) white sugar
- 1 tablespoon (7.5g) all-purpose flour
- 1 cup (244g) whole milk
- 1 teaspoon (4.3g) pure vanilla extract
- 2 tablespoons (28.25g) butter
- 1 pinch salt
- ½ cup (85g) raisins, optional

1. In a medium saucepan, heat the milk and butter until the butter has melted. Remove from heat and cool to lukewarm. Meanwhile, combine the sugar, eggs, spices, and vanilla in the bowl of a stand mixer and beat on medium speed for 1 minute. When the milk/butter mixture has cooled to lukewarm, drizzle it into the mixer and combine. Place the bread in a buttered 1½-quart casserole dish. Sprinkle with raisins, if desired. Pour the batter over the bread. Bake at 350°F for 40–45 minutes or until set. Serve warm.

2. For the sauce, mix the sugar with the flour and whisk into the milk, butter, vanilla, and salt in a medium pot on the stove. Stir constantly and bring to a boil for 3-4 minutes. Set aside for 5 minutes, then pour over warm bread pudding to serve.

# Poke Cake

*A clever mix of boxed ingredients makes this vintage recipe an easy dessert.*

1 box vanilla cake mix
One 3-ounce (85g) box Lime Jell-O
1 cup (236.59g) water, boiling
One 3-ounce (96g) box instant vanilla pudding
½ cup (65g) confectioners' sugar
2 cups (488g) milk
2 cups (150g) Homemade Whipped Cream (page 184) or Cool Whip

Prepare and bake cake mix according to package directions in a buttered 9 x 13-inch baking pan. When cake is done baking, remove from the oven and poke holes throughout with a fork. Mix the Jell-O with the boiling water and pour slowly over the cake while it is still warm. Cool completely. Meanwhile, mix the pudding with the milk and confectioners' sugar and put into the refrigerator to cool. When it has thickened, mix in 2 cups of Cool Whip or Homemade Whipped Cream (page 184) (already whipped). When cake has cooled, pour the pudding mixture over top and refrigerate.

**Note:** Flavor of cake mix, pudding, and Jell-O may be switched up as you wish.

# Grape Delight

*Clara Gingerich Miller, Dover, Delaware*

*A fresh and tasty dessert that is refreshing in summer. You can also substitute other fresh fruit.*

4 pounds red seedless grapes, washed and removed from stems, about 12 cups (1800g)
1 teaspoon (5g) lemon juice
8 ounces (226.8g) cream cheese, softened
8 ounces (226.8g) sour cream
8 ounces (226g) Cool Whip or Homemade Whipped Cream (page 184)
1½ cups (180g) confectioners' sugar

Wash the grapes and drain well. In the bowl of a stand mixer, mix the cream cheese and powdered sugar until well blended, then add the lemon juice, sour cream, and Cool Whip or Homemade Whipped Cream (page 184) (already whipped). Mix until blended, then pour over the grapes in a serving bowl.

# Date Pudding

*Esther Miller, Mt. Hope, Ohio*

*This traditional pudding always showed up during Thanksgiving or Christmas when our family gathered around the table. It is a tasty date-studded cake which is cut into small squares and layered in a trifle dish with delicious caramel sauce and Homemade Whipped Cream (page 184).*

1 cup (156g) dates, cut finely
1 cup (236.59g) boiling water
1 teaspoon (5g) baking soda
1 cup (213g) brown sugar
1 cup (120g) all-purpose flour
1 tablespoon (14g) baking powder
1 tablespoon (14.13g) butter, melted
1 large egg
Homemade Whipped Cream (page 184), for assembly

**Brown Sugar and Butter Sauce**

2 tablespoons (28.25g) butter
1 cup (213g) brown sugar
1 cup (236.59g) water
½ cup (118.29g) water mixed with 2 tablespoons (8g) Clear Jel or Thermflo and 1 tablespoon (7.5g) cornstarch
¾ teaspoon (3.25g) pure vanilla extract
½ teaspoon (2.15g) maple extract

1. Place the cut-up dates and baking soda in a heat-proof bowl and cover with the boiling water. Let it rest while you prepare the rest of the ingredients. In the bowl of a stand mixer, place the sugar, flour, baking powder, melted butter, and the egg. Pour in the date mixture and blend. Bake at 325°F in a 9 x 13-inch cake pan for about 20–25 minutes.

2. For the **Brown Sugar and Butter Sauce**: On the stovetop, heat the butter, sugar, and water to boiling. Make a slurry with ½ cup of water and the Clear Jel and cornstarch, then whisk it into the boiling mixture. Continue whisking constantly until it begins to boil again, going from cloudy to translucent. Remove from the heat and stir in the extracts. Cool.

**Assembly:** Cut the date cake into small cubes and alternate them in layers in a trifle bowl with sauce and Homemade Whipped Cream (page 184). Add bananas as garnish, if desired.

# Apple Dumpling Rollups

*Mennonite Community Cookbook (1950)*

*This recipe comes from the frayed and well-used cookbook Mother often referred to in the kitchen when she was baking or cooking. It's the first cookbook I used as a teenager, and thankfully I inherited it later during her life.*

*Apple dumplings were my father's favorite dessert, and we made them differently than a traditional dumpling wrapped in little pockets of dough. Mother rolled out the dough like for cinnamon rolls, brushed it with butter, and then poured sliced apples over it. Then, she sprinkled brown sugar and cinnamon over everything before rolling it into a log and slicing it. The slices were then placed in buttered pans and a brown sugar sauce poured over the top before sliding them into the oven to bake.*

4 cups (452g) peeled and sliced apples (about 6 whole apples of various varieties)
½ cup (106.5g) brown sugar
1 teaspoon (2.6g) ground cinnamon
4 tablespoons (56.5g) butter, melted

**Pastry Dough**

2 cups (240g) all-purpose flour
2½ teaspoons (10g) baking powder
1 teaspoon (5.69g) sea salt
⅔ cup (150.67g) unsalted butter
½ cup (122g) whole milk

**Brown Sugar Sauce**

1½ cups (390.5g) brown sugar
2 cups (473.18g) water
¼ teaspoon (0.7g) ground cinnamon
1 pinch salt
¼ cup (56.5g) unsalted butter
1 teaspoon (4.3g) pure vanilla extract

1. Peel the apples and set them aside. Whisk together the brown sugar and the cinnamon. Melt the butter. Set aside until you are ready for assembly.

2. For the **Pastry Dough**: In a medium-sized mixing bowl, sift together the flour, baking powder, and salt. Cut the butter into 1-inch square cubes and, with your hands or a pastry cutter, work it into the dry mixture. When the dough looks like coarse crumbs, pour in the milk and fold it in gently. When the dough begins to hold its shape, turn it onto a floured counter, form it into a ball, and roll it out into a rectangle shape like for cinnamon rolls. This works best if you roll it between 2 pieces of plastic wrap.

3. For the **Brown Sugar Sauce**, boil together the sugar, water, cinnamon, and salt for a few minutes, then remove from the heat and stir in the butter and vanilla.

**Assembly:** Brush the rectangle of dough with melted butter. Pour the sliced apples over the dough. Sprinkle the brown sugar and cinnamon mixture over the apples. Roll up like a cinnamon roll and slice into 1-inch-thick slices. Lay the slices into 2 buttered pie pans. Heat the brown sugar sauce and pour over the unbaked dumplings. Bake at 325°F for about 30-40 minutes until apples are tender. Serve warm with milk or ice cream.

# Cinnamon Pudding

*Esther Miller, Mt. Hope, Ohio*

*Taking a bite of this warm cinnamon cake puddled in a delicious caramel sauce is incredibly delightful, especially when topped with vanilla ice cream.*

1 cup (200g) white sugar
2 tablespoons (28.25g) butter
1 cup (244g) whole milk
1⅔ (200g) cups all-purpose flour
2 teaspoons (10g) baking powder
1 teaspoon (2.8g) cinnamon

**Brown Sugar Sauce**
1½ cups (310.5g) brown sugar
1½ cups (354.88g) cold water
2 tablespoons (28.25g) butter

1. In a small mixing bowl, whisk dry ingredients together, then stir in the milk. Pour into the bottom of a buttered 9 x 9-inch cake pan.

2. For the **Brown Sugar Sauce**: In a small saucepan, mix all ingredients together and bring to a boil.

3. Pour the Brown Sugar Sauce over the top of the cake batter in the pan. Bake at 350°F for about 20 minutes until the cake portion is done.

# Angel Food Cake Dessert

*This luscious dessert comes together quickly and looks so festive in a glass bowl. It highlights the fresh taste of strawberries paired with tender pieces of angel food cake and ribbons of Cream Cheese Whipped Cream.*

1 angel food cake, homemade or purchased from a store
Two 16-ounce (454g) packages fresh strawberries, sliced
⅓ (66g) cup white sugar

**Cream Cheese Whipped Cream**
8 ounces (226.8g) cream cheese, softened
½ cup (56.75g) confectioners' sugar
1¼ cups (300g) heavy cream

Wash, stem, and slice the strawberries. Place them in a small bowl and cover them with the sugar, stirring from time to time so they release their juices. Meanwhile, in the bowl of a stand mixer with the paddle attachment, mix the cream cheese and confectioners' sugar until blended. Scrape the bowl with a spatula. With the mixer on medium speed, slowly drizzle in the heavy cream and mix until thoroughly incorporated. Mixture will turn slightly thick like pudding.

**Assembly:** In a glass trifle bowl, loosely tear pieces of angel food cake and place in layers, starting with cake, then a layer of Cream Cheese Whipped Cream, then the strawberries. Repeat until components are used up, at least 3 layers. Also, you don't need to use all the juice in the bowl of strawberries, but it's okay to use some. Refrigerate until ready to serve. This is best eaten on the same day it is made.

# Baked Apples

*Geneva Schlabach, Sarasota, Florida*

*My mother sometimes served this instead of applesauce with supper. Often, we had it during holidays and special occasions.*

**4 large apples, peeled and quartered**
**¾ cup (159.75g) brown sugar**
**2 tablespoons (15g) all-purpose flour**
**½ teaspoon (1.3g) ground cinnamon**
**½ cup (118.29g) water**
**Whipped cream, for serving**

Line the bottom of 2 pie pans or a 9 x 13-inch cake pan with apples. Mix the sugar, flour, and cinnamon. Sprinkle over the apples. Drizzle the water over the apples to moisten. Bake at 350°F for about 40 minutes or until apples are caramelized and tender. Serve with whipped cream.

DESSERTS & SWEETS

# Apple Crisp

*Esther Miller, Mt. Hope, Ohio*

*This tastes like apple pie with half the work! The recipe does not call for cinnamon, but I sprinkled some over the apples before I added the crumb topping. Delicious with milk, whipped cream, or ice cream!*

**6 cups (750g) peeled apples, sliced or chopped**
**1 cup (200g) white sugar**
**1 cup (236.59g) water**
**2 tablespoons (14g) cornstarch**

**Crumble**
**1 cup (120g) all-purpose flour**
**¾ cup (74.25g) oats**
**1 cup (165g) brown sugar**
**½ cup (113g) melted butter**

1. Cook sugar, water, and cornstarch together until boiling, then pour over apples in a large baking dish.

2. Sprinkle crumble over the apples and bake at 350°F for about 40 minutes or until apples are tender.

# Sour Cherry Pot Pie

*An old-fashioned treat that comes together in one pot on the stovetop, this Sour Cherry Pot Pie is a recipe from our Stutzman family that has been passed down through several generations. It can be eaten for breakfast or dinner. Growing up, we always served it with milk or cream. The quick recipe for the dumplings comes from the back of the Bisquick® box.*

**4 cups (616g) sour cherries, frozen and pitted**
**4 cups (946.35g) water**
**1 cup (213g) brown sugar**
**¼ teaspoon (1.42g) sea salt**
**2 cups (312g) Bisquick**
**⅔ cup (166g) milk**
**1 tablespoon (14.13g) softened butter**

In a large kettle, bring the cherries, water, and brown sugar to a boil. Combine the Bisquick, milk, and softened butter, stirring with a fork until a soft dough forms. Drop the dough by the teaspoon into the boiling cherry mixture. Make sure the cherry mixture continues boiling while you are spooning in the dough. When all the dough is in the pot, boil uncovered for 5 more minutes. Reduce heat to low, cover, and cook for an additional 15 minutes until the dumplings are cooked through. Remove from heat and allow to cool for about 10 minutes before serving. Spoon into bowls and add milk, if desired.

# Brown Sugar Pudding

*While my siblings grew up with the German pudding mother called* brei, *I was more familiar with the version she made with brown sugar by the time I was a teenager. It is a sweeter version of* brei *and carries a caramelized flavor. Delicious eaten warm, or used to layer with graham crackers, bananas, and whipped cream for graham cracker pudding.*

**4½ cups (1098g) milk, divided**
**½ cup (60g) all-purpose flour**
**1 cup (213g) brown sugar**
**1 cup (200g) white sugar**
**3 large eggs, beaten slightly**
**½ teaspoon (2.84g) salt**
**1 tablespoon (13g) pure vanilla extract**

In a medium saucepan, heat 4 cups (976g) of milk to steaming. Meanwhile, in a medium mixing bowl, stir together the flour, sugar, and salt. In another bowl, whisk the eggs with ½ cup (122g) milk until smooth, then whisk into the dry ingredients. When the milk on stovetop begins to steam, whisk in the egg yolk/brown sugar mixture and continue whisking constantly until pudding thickens and comes to a boil. Remove from heat and add vanilla extract, stirring to combine. Pour into bowls to eat warm, or cool to use for graham cracker pudding. If placing in the refrigerator to cool, place a layer of wax paper or plastic wrap directly on top of the pudding in order to prevent a skin from forming as it cools.

*You can make these ahead of time and freeze in an airtight container until you need them for a party.*

# Pecan Tarts

*An irresistible handheld treat that's perfect for holiday parties, these tarts taste like mini pecan pies.*

**Crust**
- 2 cups (240g) all-purpose flour
- 2 sticks (226.8g) butter, softened
- 6 ounces (170.1g) cream cheese, softened

**Pecan Filling**
- 3 large eggs
- 1 cup (340g) maple syrup
- ½ cup (106.5g) brown sugar
- ¼ teaspoon (1.42g) sea salt
- 1 teaspoon (4.3g) pure vanilla extract
- 1 tablespoon (14.13g) butter, melted
- ¾ cup (163.5g) finely chopped pecans

1. To make the **Crust**, combine the butter and cream cheese in the bowl of a stand mixer. Slowly add the flour and mix until incorporated. Turn dough onto a floured counter and form into a disc. Wrap in plastic wrap and refrigerate for 10 minutes. Divide the dough into 4 equal pieces and then roll each piece into a log. Cut each log into 8 pieces. You will now have 32 pieces. Press each piece into the bottom and up the sides of a muffin tin. If you only have one tin (24 muffins), you can refrigerate half the dough until the first batch is done baking. When you have formed the dough in each tin, place them into the refrigerator to chill while you mix up the Pecan Filling.

2. For the **Pecan Filling**: In the bowl of a stand mixer, beat the eggs, and then add the maple syrup, brown sugar, salt, vanilla, and melted butter. Blend well.

**Assembly:** Place a teaspoon (or less) of crushed nuts in each tart and add the filling. Bake at 375°F for 10 minutes, then reduce heat to 350°F and bake for 10 minutes longer, or until golden brown. Makes 32 tarts.

# Chocolate Dessert Cake

*An old-fashioned dessert reminiscent of the Ho Hos® Snack Cake, featuring a layer of moist chocolate cake topped with a creamy filling and covered in a decadent chocolate ganache.*

- ½ cup (122g) milk
- ½ tablespoon (7.5g) vinegar
- ½ cup (108.59g) oil
- 1 cup (200g) white sugar
- 1 large egg
- 1¼ cups (150g) all-purpose flour
- 1 teaspoon (6g) baking soda
- ¼ teaspoon (1.23g) salt
- ¼ cup (21.25g) cocoa powder
- ½ teaspoon (2.15g) pure vanilla extract
- ½ cup (118.29g) hot water

**Cream Topping**

- ¼ cup (30g) all-purpose flour
- 1¼ cups (305g) milk
- 1 cup (205g) Crisco
- ½ cup (113g) butter, softened to room temperature
- ½ cup (100g) white sugar
- ½ cup (62.5g) confectioners' sugar
- ¼ cup (24g) marshmallow crème

**Chocolate Ganache**

- ¾ cup (172.5g) heavy cream
- 1¼ cups (212.50g) semi-sweet chocolate chips

1. In a glass measuring cup, mix the milk with the vinegar and set aside. In the bowl of a stand mixer, blend together the oil and sugar, then add the egg and beat until blended. Whisk together the flour, baking soda, salt, and cocoa powder and add to the mixer, along with the milk, vinegar, and hot water. Scrape the bowl, add the vanilla, and whip for 1 minute until blended. Pour batter into a buttered and floured 9 x 9-inch square cake pan. Bake at 350°F for approximately 25–30 minutes until a toothpick inserted comes out clean. Cool.

2. For the **Cream Topping**: In a small saucepan, measure out the flour and drizzle in the milk while whisking constantly until there is a smooth consistency. Turn the heat to medium and continue whisking constantly until the mixture thickens. Remove from the heat, place into a bowl, and put in the refrigerator to cool. Place a piece of plastic wrap directly over the mixture while cooling. While this is cooling, in the bowl of a stand mixer, whip the Crisco and the butter until creamy. Add the sugar and confectioners' sugar and whip again. When the flour mixture has cooled in the fridge, add it to the mixer, a tablespoon at a time, along with the marshmallow crème and whip until fluffy and fully incorporated. Smooth over the chocolate cake.

3. For the **Chocolate Ganache**: In the medium saucepan, heat the milk until it is bubbling around the edges. Remove from the heat and immediately pour the chocolate chips into the cream. Cover with a lid and allow to rest for about 8 minutes, then stir briskly to combine until the ganache is completely incorporated and smooth. Allow ganache to come to room temperature before smoothing over the cream layer to complete the dessert.

# Brown Betty

*Ruth Rabatin, Millersburg, Ohio*

*The nutty flavor of wholegrain spelt flour and the raw cane sugar combine to make this a healthier option for an apple dessert. Traditionally, an apple Betty has a crumb mixture layered throughout the fruit, but you can also put the apples in the bottom and the crumbs on top.*

- 7 cups (763g) peeled and chopped apples (about 6 large apples)
- 2 cups (198g) oats
- 2 cups (220g) spelt flour
- 1 cup (210g) of coconut oil or olive oil
- ½ teaspoon (3g) baking soda
- 1 cup (220g) raw sugar
- Ground cinnamon, to taste
- Pumpkin pie spice, to taste
- 3 tablespoons (42.38g) butter, cut into small chunks

Pour apples into a buttered 9 x 13-inch pan. Scatter the chunks of butter over the apples, then sprinkle with cinnamon and pumpkin pie spice. In a medium mixing bowl, whisk together the oats, flour, baking soda, and sugar. Then, add the oil and mix well. Pour over the apples. Sprinkle with more cinnamon and pumpkin pie spice. Bake at 350°F for about 40 minutes, or until apples are tender and cake is baked. This is delicious served with a little cream or milk poured over it in a bowl.

# Lime Jell-O Pudding

*One of my son's favorite desserts, this pudding carries an interesting texture because of the cottage cheese. You can also use other flavors of Jell-O, such as orange or lemon.*

- One 16-ounce (453g) container cottage cheese
- One 3-ounce (85g) box Lime Jell-O
- One 20-ounce can (567g) crushed pineapple, drained
- One 11-ounce (311g) can mandarin oranges, drained
- One 8-ounce (226g) container Cool Whip, or 2 cups Homemade Whipped Cream (page 184)

In a large bowl, combine the cottage cheese with the Jell-O. Then, stir in the pineapple and mandarin oranges. Lastly, fold in the Cool Whip or Homemade Whipped Cream (page 184) and stir until blended. Pour into a bowl and refrigerate. Serve chilled.

# Grandma's Chocolate Pudding

*Naomi Rabatin, Millersburg, Ohio*

*This recipe fills a large trifle bowl and is great for a crowd of people around your dinner table. It is delicious when scooped into bowls and served warm, or you can chill and then add whipped cream when ready to serve.*

**1 gallon (3.79L) whole milk**
**2 cups (404g) white sugar**
**1¾ cup (148.75g) cocoa powder**
**1 generous pinch salt**
**4 large eggs, fork-beaten**
**2 cups (240g) all-purpose flour**
**1 teaspoon (5g) pure vanilla extract**

1. Heat 3 quarts (2.84 liters) of milk in a large pot on the stovetop until skin forms over the top. Meanwhile in a large bowl, mix all the dry ingredients together. Then, add the fork-beaten eggs and stir in 1 quart of milk. Whisk until the mixture is smooth.

2. When the milk on the stovetop is ready, remove from the burner and add the chocolate mixture from the mixing bowl. Whisk thoroughly, then place the pot back onto the burner over medium heat and whisk constantly until the pudding starts to boil. Allow to boil for 1 minute, stirring constantly, then remove from the heat and add the vanilla extract. Let cool briefly, then pour into a large glass serving bowl. Serve with whipped cream.

# Banana Pudding

*Sara Mae Stutzman, Dover, Ohio*

*Everyone loves banana pudding, and this recipe by Eagle Brand has sweetened condensed milk and instant vanilla pudding, making it a quick and easy version to make. Many cooks have used this recipe over the years.*

**1½ cups (353g) cold water**
**One 14-ounce (396g) can Eagle Brand sweetened condensed milk**
**One 3.4-ounce (96g) package instant vanilla pudding**
**2 cups (496g) heavy cream, whipped**
**2 teaspoons (10g) pure vanilla extract**
**1 pinch salt**
**One 11-ounce (311g) box mini vanilla wafers (you will use about half the box)**
**4 bananas, sliced and swished around in lemon juice to keep from browning**

In the bowl of a stand mixer, combine the milk and the water. Add the pudding mix and beat well. Chill for 5 minutes. Meanwhile, whip the cream to stiff peaks, add the vanilla extract and salt, and then fold into the chilled pudding.

**Assembly:** Spoon 1 cup of pudding mixture into a glass serving bowl. Layer with wafers, bananas, and pudding. Keep layering until you end with pudding. Chill. Garnish as desired.

**Note:** Vanilla wafers may be whole or crushed. I left them whole for a trifle layered look.

# Caramel Corn

*Popcorn covered in an easy boiled caramel glaze is a wonderful snack to have on hand during the holidays. It's made with maple syrup, so there's no high fructose corn syrup, which is always a win!*

**8 quarts (256g) popped corn**
**2 cups (426g) brown sugar**
**1 cup (226g) butter**
**½ cup (156g) maple syrup**
**1 teaspoon (5.69g) salt**
**1 teaspoon (4.3g) pure vanilla extract**
**½ teaspoon (3g) baking soda**

Pop the corn and pour into a large mixing bowl. In a medium saucepan, place the brown sugar, butter, maple syrup, and salt. Stir until it starts to boil, then don't stir anymore. When it comes to a rolling boil, let it boil for 4–5 minutes. Remove from the heat and stir in the vanilla and baking soda. Pour over the popped corn and mix thoroughly with a large spoon or spatula. Pour into a large roaster or place on 2 large baking pans. Bake in the oven at 250°F for 1 hour, stirring every 15 minutes. Then, let cool and store in an airtight container.

# Peach Delight

*This is a dessert my mother-in-law often serves during the summer when all the family comes home for dinner. She likes to use the ready-made peach glaze you can buy at the grocery store, which she mixes with freshly sliced peaches. Whether you make it from scratch or use store-bought peach glaze for the topping, it will be delicious!*

**Graham Cracker Crust**
**1½ cups (206g) crushed graham crackers**
**3 tablespoons (42.38g) butter, melted**
**¼ cup (41.25g) white sugar**

**Cream Cheese Filling**
**8 ounces (226.8g) cream cheese**
**½ cup (55g) white sugar**
**1¾ cups (434g) heavy cream**

***Peach Compote: Page 189***

1. In a bowl, mix the ingredients for the **Graham Cracker Crust** together and spread them into the bottom of a 9 x 13-inch pan. Chill while you make the rest of the ingredients.

2. For the **Cream Cheese Filling**: In the bowl of a stand mixer, whip the cream cheese and the sugar together until blended and smooth. Slowly, with the mixer on medium speed, drizzle the cream down the inside of the bowl. Scrape the bowl occasionally. When all the cream has been incorporated, whip the mixture to stiff peaks, and then pour over top of the graham cracker crust.

3. For the **Peach Compote**, see page 189. When this mixture has cooled, pour it over top of the cream cheese mixture in the pan.

# Peach Cobbler

*Amish Community Cookbook*

*Spooning out steaming bowls of fresh-from-the-oven peach cobbler for your guests is a delicious way to end a late summer meal. Topped with vanilla ice cream or whipped cream, it is an easy dessert that quickly warms the heart.*

**Peaches**

6 cups (900g) peeled and sliced peaches
¾ cup (1485g) white sugar
2 tablespoons (15g) all-purpose flour
½ teaspoon (1.32g) ground cinnamon
¼ teaspoon (1.42g) sea salt
1 teaspoon (4.34g) pure vanilla extract
1 tablespoon (14.13g) melted butter

**Cobbler**

1 cup (120g) all-purpose flour
1 cup (200g) white sugar
1 teaspoon (4g) baking powder
½ teaspoon (2.84g) sea salt
4 tablespoons (56.5g) butter, melted
2 large eggs, slightly beaten
2 tablespoons (24.75g) white or raw sugar for sprinkling over dough

1. For the **Peaches**, mix the ingredients and pour into a buttered 9 x 13-inch pan.

2. For the **Cobbler**, mix ingredients and drop by the spoonful onto the Peaches. Sprinkle with white or raw sugar. Bake at 350°F for about 30 minutes until Peach Cobbler is done. Serve warm with ice cream or whipped cream.

DESSERTS & SWEETS

# Blueberry Cobbler

*This easy cobbler has a base of fresh blueberry pie filling topped with craggy biscuits and baked in a 12-inch cast iron skillet. When eaten with milk or ice cream, it is the ultimate bowl of comfort food.*

**Blueberry Pie Filling**

4 cups (600g) fresh blueberries
⅔ cup (134.66g) white sugar
2 tablespoons (14g) cornstarch
Zest and juice of 1 lime

**Biscuits**

2 cups (240g) all-purpose flour
2½ teaspoons (9.5g) baking powder
2 teaspoons (8.25g) white sugar
¾ teaspoon (4.27g) salt
1½ cups (360g) heavy cream
Course sugar and melted butter for the tops

1. For the **Blueberry Pie Filling**, mix all together in a bowl and pour into the bottom of a buttered 12-inch cast iron skillet.

2. For the **Biscuits**: In a medium bowl, whisk the flour, baking soda, sugar, and salt together. Pour in the cream and gently fold in with a spatula just until blended. Don't overmix! Drop the dough with a cookie scoop onto the blueberry mixture in the skillet. Brush the biscuits with melted butter and sprinkle them with coarse sugar. Bake the skillet at 375°F for about 30-40 minutes depending on the size of biscuits. Serve with milk, whipped cream, or ice cream.

# Blueberry Delight

*This Blueberry Delight is made with a shortbread crust, a middle layer of cream cheese whipped cream, and topped with fresh Blueberry Compote. While the quintessential Amish dessert is most likely Cherry Delight, this blueberry cousin is equally delicious.*

**Crust**

1 cup (226g) unsalted butter, room temperature
½ cup (55g) confectioners' sugar
2½ cups (300g) all-purpose flour
1 teaspoon (5.68g) sea salt

**Second Layer**

8 ounces (226.8g) cream cheese, room temperature
1 cup (110g) confectioners' sugar
1 teaspoon (5g) pure vanilla extract
2 cups (150g) Homemade Whipped Cream

***Homemade Whipped Cream: Page 184***

***Blueberry Compote: Page 190***

1. To make the **Crust**: In the bowl of a stand mixer, beat butter and sugar together. Add flour and salt and mix until crumbly. Press into the bottom of a 9 x 12-inch pan and bake at 350°F for about 20 minutes. Cool, then add the second layer.

2. For the **Second Layer**: In the bowl of a stand mixer, beat the cream cheese, confectioners' sugar, vanilla, and salt until it is smooth. Then, gradually add the whipped cream and mix until blended. Pour this mixture over the cooled crust.

3. To make the **Homemade Whipped Cream**, see page 184.

4. For the **Blueberry Compote**: see page 190. When cooled, pour this mixture as the final topping over the second layer. Refrigerate. Serve when well chilled.

# Graham Cracker Cream Pudding

*A prominent dessert of dinner buffets in Amish-style restaurants, this Graham Cracker Cream Pudding is simple and tasty.*

**Graham Cracker Crust**

1½ cups (206g) crushed graham crackers
3 tablespoons (42.38g) butter, melted
¼ cup (41.25g) brown sugar

**Cream Pudding Filling**

2¾ cups (671g) whole milk, divided
¾ cup (151.59g) white sugar
½ teaspoon (2.84g) sea salt
3 tablespoons (21g) cornstarch
4 large egg yolks, beaten
3 tablespoons (42.38g) unsalted butter
2 teaspoons (10g) pure vanilla extract

1. For the **Graham Cracker Crust**, mix ingredients together and press into bottom and sides of a 9-inch (23cm) pie pan. Bake at 350°F for 8 minutes. Cool.

2. For the **Cream Pudding Filling**, heat 2 cups of milk. Meanwhile in a medium bowl, whisk together ½ cup (61g) milk, sugar, salt, and beaten egg yolks. In a small bowl, make a slurry of the cornstarch and the remaining ¼ cup (30.5g) of milk. When the milk on the stovetop is almost steaming, whisk in the milk/sugar/egg mixture, stirring constantly, then drizzle in the slurry of cornstarch and milk. Whisk continuously until the pudding begins to bubble. Let it boil for close to a minute, then remove from heat and stir in the butter and vanilla. Pour into a bowl to cool slightly before pouring into the 9-inch (23cm) graham cracker crust.

3. Chill for at least 4 hours, then cover with whipped cream, garnish with graham cracker crumbs, and serve.

# Oreo Ice Cream Pudding

*This recipe has been a family favorite since our kids were little. Every Sunday night we would go to Grandma and Grandpa Gingerich's house where all the cousins would play together while the grownups talked in the living room. Usually, someone brought Oreo Ice Cream Pudding, and to the happy cheers of the children, it was scooped into bowls and passed around.*

1 lb. 2.12 oz. (513g) bag Oreo Cookies, crushed
2 quarts (1.89 L) vanilla ice cream

**Whipped Cream**
1½ cups (368g) heavy whipping cream
⅓ cup (36.6g) confectioners' sugar
1 teaspoon (5g) pure vanilla extract

1. Place the vanilla ice cream in a large mixing bowl to let it melt a bit.

2. To make the **Whipped Cream**, place the cream, sugar, and vanilla into the bowl of a stand mixer and mix until it reaches stiff peaks.

3. Add the Whipped Cream and two-thirds of the crushed Oreos to the large mixing bowl. Mix all together and pour into a 9 x 12-inch pan. Cover with the rest of the crushed Oreos and freeze for several hours until firm. Remove from freezer 15 minutes prior to serving.

# Ice Cream Cookie Sandwiches

*This delicious hand-held dessert uses components from two recipes in this book, the Best-Ever Chocolate Chip Cookies (page 110) and the Oreo Ice Cream Pudding (above). Both items can be made ahead of time and then assembled at the last minute. Alternately, you can assemble them and then wrap them tightly in plastic wrap and place them in the freezer until you are ready to serve them. It is the perfect treat on a hot summer night sitting on the front porch, or to serve at birthday parties.*

**To assemble the Ice Cream Cookie Sandwiches:** Place half of the cookies (or as many as you want to make) upside down on the counter. Scoop a generous serving of Oreo Ice Cream Pudding onto each one using a medium-sized cookie scoop, then cover with the remaining cookies. It's important to let the pudding thaw briefly so the cookies won't break when you push them together. Serve immediately, or wrap individually in plastic wrap and freeze.

# Grandma's Fudge

*Grandma Linda Gingerich, Millersburg, Ohio*

*The original recipe for this fantastic fudge used to appear on the back of a Kraft® marshmallow creme jar. It is a classic Christmas treat our family enjoys each holiday season.*

- 3 cups (594g) white sugar
- ¾ cup (169.5g) butter
- 6 ounces (170.09g) evaporated milk
- One 12-ounce (340.19g) package semi-sweet chocolate chips
- 7 ounces (200g) marshmallow crème
- 1 cup (120g) chopped walnuts
- 1 teaspoon (4.3g) vanilla extract

1. Line a 9 x 9-inch pan with foil or parchment paper.

2. Bring the sugar, butter, and evaporated milk to a boil. Cook for 7–8 minutes, stirring constantly. When finished, add vanilla, marshmallow crème, chocolate chips, and nuts. Stir until blended. Pour into the pan and cool. Cut into tiny squares to serve.

# Louie and Honey's Hot Chocolate Mix

*A cup of hot chocolate warms up any cold day, and this recipe makes it easy! Made with 70% dark chocolate chips and decadent Cacao Barry powder, it mixes up quickly in the blender to make ahead for those cozy winter evenings. Top it with whipped cream or marshmallows or both!*

- ½ cup (84.5g) 70% dark chocolate chips
- ½ cup (104g) white sugar
- ¼ cup (29g) confectioners' sugar
- ½ cup (58g) Cacao Barry cocoa powder
- 1 pinch salt

1. Place all ingredients in a blender or food processor and blend until incorporated. Store in an airtight container for several months.

2. To make hot chocolate: Use 3 tablespoons of the mix for every 8 ounces of hot milk. Top with whipped cream, marshmallows, and chocolate shavings.

# Chocolate Cookie Pudding

*This pudding is sometimes known as dirt pudding and is fun to decorate with gummy worms. It is a kid's favorite.*

**Pudding**

2¾ cups (385g) whole milk, divided
¾ cup (151.5g) white sugar
½ teaspoon (2.84g) sea salt
3 tablespoons (21g) cornstarch
4 large egg yolks, beaten
3 tablespoons (42.38g) unsalted butter
2 teaspoons (10g) pure vanilla extract

**Cookie Crumble**

1 lb. 2.12 oz. (513g) Oreo cookies, crushed
½ stick (56.5g) of butter, melted

**Whipped Cream Cheese**

8 ounces (226.8g) cream cheese
1 cup (165g) confectioners' sugar
1½ cups (359.85g) heavy whipping cream
1 teaspoon (5g) pure vanilla extract

1. For the **Pudding**, heat 2 cups (488g) of milk. Meanwhile in a medium bowl, whisk together ½ cup (61g) milk, sugar, salt, and beaten egg yolks. In a small bowl, make a slurry of the cornstarch and the remaining ¼ cup (30.5g) of milk. When the milk on the stovetop is almost steaming, whisk in the milk/sugar/egg mixture, stirring constantly, then drizzle in the slurry of cornstarch and milk. Whisk continuously until the pudding begins to bubble and thicken. Let it boil for close to a minute, then remove from heat and stir in the butter and vanilla. Pour into a bowl to cool.

2. To make the **Cookie Crumble**, combine crushed cookies and butter in a bowl and set aside.

3. For the **Whipped Cream Cheese**: In the bowl of a stand mixer, whip the cream cheese and confectioners' sugar until blended. Scrape the bowl. Slowly drizzle in the heavy cream, a little bit at a time, and then whip until it reaches stiff peaks. Whisk in vanilla extract.

**Assembly:** When the pudding has chilled, stir in the Whipped Cream Cheese mixture until blended, then stir in the Cookie Crumbs, reserving some cookie crumbs for the top. Pour into a 9 x 13-inch pan, top with crumbs, and chill thoroughly before serving.

# Schooling

*Amish students go to school from ages 6 through 14 or 15, (1st through 8th grade). They meet in a one-room schoolhouse along with about 30–35 other students—generally their siblings or cousins—that is usually within walking distance of their home. Generally, you will also see a softball or baseball field, as well as some playground equipment and outhouses. The school day starts promptly at 8:30 AM with a bible reading, reciting the Lord's Prayer, and singing hymns. While at school, the students also do chores to learn responsibility, like cleaning the chalkboards, bringing in firewood, sweeping the floors, emptying the trash can, and wiping desks. They do not learn "religion" at school because the Amish consider that to be the parents' responsibility.*

Some Mennonite churches also have their own schools, although many use the public school system. I was permitted to attend public school for grades one to three, mostly because my older brother was a teacher there. For grades four through eight, I attended a private Mennonite school.

When it comes to higher education, Amish children are generally prohibited from attending high school or college, but most Mennonite churches do allow education past the eighth grade. The church I attended was a conservative Mennonite congregation that sided with the Amish Church in this view. This meant that school was done for me after eighth grade. My hunger for learning never diminished, though, and I educated myself through devouring books, and in my teen years by traveling in Europe. Years later, at the age of 46, I fulfilled a life-long dream of attending college.

## Teaching in an Amish School

*The teacher at an Amish school is usually an unmarried Amish woman between the ages of 18 and 22, who also has only an eighth grade education. She teaches all eight grades by herself, but many times the older students help by teaching the younger ones. Sometimes, depending on the size of the school, an assistant is assigned to the teacher. The teacher is expected to teach reading, math, writing, and penmanship, but also history, geography, social studies, art, and science. She must also teach High German and English. The Amish base their education on societal values, emphasizing collaboration and cooperation. They discourage competition and studying ahead in the curriculum without one's peers.*

One of the private Amish schools in Mt. Hope, Ohio, where I taught all eight grades for three years.

I spent four years teaching in a one-room Amish school in my early twenties. From firing up the big coal furnace each day in the winter, to teaching all eight grades in multiple subjects daily, to playing softball on the playground at recess, those were some of the most challenging and rewarding years. The school day began with the ringing of the big bell in the tower. The students came walking across the fields and roads of the surrounding community, swinging lunch pails and chatting happily. Girls in their bonnets and boys in their straw hats, faces and hands scrubbed clean after morning chores in the barn. Lessons were learned, songs were sung, and stories were read, but I think their favorite was the Christmas play we did each year.

Now those students have all grown up with families of their own. Some of them went on to become teachers in Amish schools while others have settled into the familiar rhythm of life on the farm. Some own small businesses, and others work in local factories. But I like to think they will always carry a little bit of my heart and influence into their lives from those years we spent together in that one-room school.

# CHAPTER 4

Going to Aunt Elizabeth's farm as a child carried an air of anticipation and adventure I craved. The only one of my father's nine siblings who remained in the Amish church, Elizabeth and her husband, Dan, lived on a farm complete with an 1800s house and barn, which became my favorite childhood haunts. Compared to our own farm, Elizabeth's farm had no electricity. The barn with its old sandstones and timbers was dimly lit by kerosene lanterns during winter's darker hours and always smelled of horses and leather.

The house had no modern appliances, and besides having no electricity, Elizabeth cooked over a wood-fired stove. This was fascinating to me as she lifted the lid to throw a couple pieces of chopped wood into the firebox and I watched the flames leap around them eagerly. Soon, whatever she was cooking on the stovetop began to sizzle and pop as the fire was stoked into a vibrant blaze. But the most exciting feature of the house was in the basement where a low stone trough held creek water, which was piped into the cellar. There was an overflow pipe, so that the water was always running and always fresh and cold. Since there was no refrigerator, only an icebox upstairs, this trough provided cold storage for food year-round.

Nearly as exciting as the creek in the cellar was Elizabeth's pantry. We visited her farm often when I was growing up and spent many an evening around the dinner table with their family. After dinner, while the adults chatted around the table, I would slide out of my chair and tiptoe across the creaking wood floor through the door of the old kitchen pantry. By the light of the moon shining through the single-paned window, my hands found the shelves holding rows of old tins. Breathlessly, I reached to uncover the magic: some held cookies, others candy, and some a disappointing assortment of kitchen odds and ends. When my fingers found the cookies, I would chuckle as I gathered a generous handful. Sitting cross-legged on the worn wooden floor, I ate them one by one as the voices droned on and lanterns flickered and hissed in the kitchen.

I owe my love of cookies to Aunt Elizabeth. There were molasses cookies, fruit-topped cookies, date-filled cookies, and simple Amish Church Cookies (page 114). And then at Christmas came the frosted sugar cookies with sprinkles that I loved to dip in hot chocolate. I don't remember eating chocolate chip cookies at her house, but my passion for those developed years later.

While Elizabeth has long since passed on, her daughters still live on the farmstead and carry on her traditions of hospitality and delicious cooking. The old house has been replaced with a new one and modernized with updated appliances, including a refrigerator and a gas stove. The creek water trough is gone, but there is still no electricity. It is powered by solar energy, which many of the Amish in Holmes County, Ohio are now using.

Still, the memories are strong within those walls. Now when I visit, it's a joy to see my grandsons making memories of their own as they sit at the table for a treat from the pantry, or romp through the barn where the smell of kerosene is gone, but the nostalgic scent of horses and old leather remains. And I can be sure that somewhere there is likely a tin of cookies waiting to be discovered.

## • RECIPES •

# Cookies, Brownies & Bars

# How to Make Raisin Crème Whoopie Pies

*Clara Gingerich Miller, Dover, Delaware*



## Ingredients

1 cup (226g) butter, softened to room temperature
1 cup (200g) white sugar
1 cup (213g) brown sugar
3 large eggs
1 teaspoon (4.3g) pure vanilla extract
1 teaspoon (6g) baking soda
¼ teaspoon (1.42g) salt
3½ cups (420g) all-purpose flour
½ cup (122g) milk
1 cup (170g) raisins

***Crème Filling: Page 186***

**1.** Gather all the ingredients you will need to make the whoopie pie batter.

**2.** In the bowl of a stand mixer, cream together the butter and sugars for about 3–4 minutes until fluffy, scraping the bowl. Add the eggs and vanilla, beating to incorporate. Then, whisk together the baking soda, salt, and flour and add to the mixer, alternately with the milk. Scrape the bowl. Last, fold in the raisins.

**3.** Line baking sheets with parchment paper and scoop out the cookie dough using a 2-inch scoop.

**4.** Bake the cookies at 350°F for about 8–9 minutes. They will be just slightly golden around the edges. It's important not to overbake them, as they will continue to bake on the pan when removed from the oven.

**5.** After cooling them on the pan for about 5 minutes, remove them from the pan to cool completely, alternating them with bottoms facing up and down. Make the Crème Filling (page 186) while the cookies are cooling.

**6.** Place 1 scoop of filling on each cookie with bottom facing up.

**7.** Press a cookie on top, pushing down gently to spread the filling to the edges.

**8.** Continue until all cookie sandwiches have been assembled. Store in an airtight container or wrap individually in plastic wrap.

# Whoopie Pies

*Sometimes called Gobs in Pennsylvania, this recipe from my childhood in Ohio is also popular in Maine. Regardless of where it comes from, the whoopie pie is a beloved chocolate cake-like sandwich cookie with a delightful cream filling. At our bakery, we like to use Salted Caramel Buttercream (page 181) or Peppermint Buttercream (page 187) for the filling, although a vanilla cream filling is traditional (Crème Filling, page 186).*

**2 cups (240g) all-purpose flour**
**¼ cup (21.25g) cocoa powder**
**1 teaspoon (6g) baking soda**
**1 teaspoon (5.69g) sea salt**
**1 cup (224g) buttermilk**
**1 teaspoon (4.2g) vanilla**
**8 tablespoons (113g) butter, softened**
**1 cup (213g) brown sugar, packed**
**1 large egg**
**⅓ cup (78.86g) hot water**

In a medium bowl, whisk together the flour, cocoa powder, baking soda, and salt until combined. In a small bowl, whisk together the buttermilk and vanilla. Next, in the bowl of a stand mixer, beat the sugar and the butter on medium-high until pale and fluffy, about 3 minutes. Then, add the egg and beat until combined. Scrape the bowl and reduce speed to low, alternating the dry ingredients with the buttermilk mixture, beginning and ending with the dry mixture. Lastly, add the hot water. Scrape sides of bowl occasionally and mix until smooth. With a 2-inch cookie scoop, portion out the dough onto parchment-lined cookie sheets. Bake for about 8-10 minutes at 350°F. Place cookies on a cooling rack until cool, then turn upside down and place a scoop of your favorite filling on a cookie and top with another. Continue until you have all the cookie sandwiches assembled. Yields approximately 10 sandwiches.

# Oatmeal Spelt Cookies

*Ruth Rabatin, Millersburg, Ohio*

*These cookies are a healthier version made with spelt, an ancient grain packed with fiber and other nutrient-rich whole grains.*

2 sticks (227g) butter
¾ cup (123.75g) brown sugar
¾ cup (150g) white sugar
2 large eggs
1 teaspoon (5g) vanilla
1½ cups (180g) spelt flour
1 teaspoon (5.68g) sea salt
1 teaspoon (6g) baking soda
3 cups (297g) oats

Cream the butter until soft and fluffy. Add the sugar and beat again until creamed. Scrape the bowl, then add the eggs, beating after each addition. Add the vanilla and mix for about 1 minute. In a separate bowl, whisk together the flour, salt, and baking soda and add to the cookie mixture. Last, add the oats. Beat until blended. Bake at 350°F for about 10-12 minutes. Yields approximately 16–20 cookies.

# Peanut Butter Chocolate Chip Cookies

*These cookies have been a favorite in our family since our children were little. They've come with us on every family vacation and are a top seller at the bakery. Easy to make with no fussy ingredients, they turn out great every time.*

1 cup (226g) unsalted butter, softened
1 cup (270g) Smucker's® Natural Creamy Peanut Butter
1 cup (200g) white sugar
1 cup (165g) brown sugar
2 large eggs
2½ (300g) cups all-purpose flour
1½ teaspoons (9g) baking soda
1 teaspoon (4g) baking powder
½ teaspoon (2.84g) salt
2 cups (350g) semi-sweet chocolate chips

1. Cream butter, peanut butter, and sugars together. Add eggs, one at a time, and beat until blended. Combine dry ingredients and add to creamed mixture just until clumps of flour disappear. Stir in chocolate chips.

2. With a medium-sized scoop, portion out cookie dough onto a baking sheet lined with parchment paper. Bake at 350°F for 16 minutes (rotating pan halfway through bake time). Do not overbake. Remove from oven and let the cookies cool on the baking rack for 10 minutes before removing to wire rack to cool. Yields 24-26 cookies.

# Best-Ever Chocolate Chip Cookies

*Amish Community Cookbook*

1 cup (226g) unsalted butter
1 cup (165g) brown sugar
½ cup (100g) white sugar
1 teaspoon (4.34g) pure vanilla extract
2 large eggs
2 cups (240g) all-purpose flour
1 teaspoon (6g) baking soda
½ teaspoon (2.84g) sea salt
1½ cups (255g) semi-sweet or dark chocolate chips
Flake sea salt for garnish

In the bowl of a stand mixer, mix the butter and sugar until creamy, about 4 minutes. Meanwhile, whisk the flour, baking soda, and salt in a bowl and set aside. Add the eggs, one at a time, and then the vanilla to the sugar/butter mixture and beat until incorporated. Add the dry ingredients and beat until blended, then stir in the chocolate chips. Chill cookie dough for about 30 minutes, then scoop into balls and bake on cookie sheets lined with parchment paper. Bake for about 10-12 minutes, until cookies are turning golden around the edges and tops are no longer wet. Do not overbake. Let them rest on the baking tray for about 15 minutes before moving to a cooling rack. Garnish with flake sea salt. Yields approximately 20 cookies.

# Gingersnap Cookies

*Amish Community Cookbook*

*These gingerbread cookies can either be rolled out as cut-outs for a crunchier taste, or can be rolled into balls, dipped in sugar, and baked for a chewy texture. Either way, they are filled with warm spices and perfect for the holidays.*

- ¾ cup (169.5g) melted butter
- 1 cup (200g) white sugar, plus additional for rolling
- 1 large egg, beaten
- 3 tablespoons (60g) sorghum or molasses
- 2 cups (24g) all-purpose flour
- 1½ teaspoons (9g) baking soda
- 1 teaspoon (2.6g) ground cinnamon
- ½ teaspoon (1.3g) cloves
- ½ teaspoon 1.3g) ground ginger
- ¼ teaspoon (0.65g) cardamom

In the bowl of a stand mixer, cream together the butter and sugar. Add the egg and molasses, scraping the bowl. Whisk together the dry ingredients and add to the mixer. Form into small balls and roll in sugar. Bake at 350°F for about 9–10 minutes. (A longer bake yields a crispier cookie.) Alternatively, the dough can be rolled out between 2 pieces of plastic wrap, refrigerated overnight, and cut into gingerbread shapes the next day and baked at 350°F for 10–12 minutes. Yields approximately 20 round cookies.

# Cakebox Cookies

*These cookies are rich and fudgy from the chocolate cake mix in addition to chocolate chips. They are easy to make and were a favorite of my kids growing up.*

- 1 box chocolate cake mix
- 2 large eggs
- ½ cup (108.32g) oil
- 2 tablespoons (29.57g) water
- 1½ cups (255g) chocolate chips

In a medium-sized mixing bowl, combine all ingredients and stir together until incorporated. Drop by the spoonful onto a baking sheet lined with parchment paper. Bake at 350°F for about 10 minutes. Do not overbake. Remove from oven and allow to rest on cookie sheet for several minutes before moving to a cooling rack. Yields 16–20 cookies.

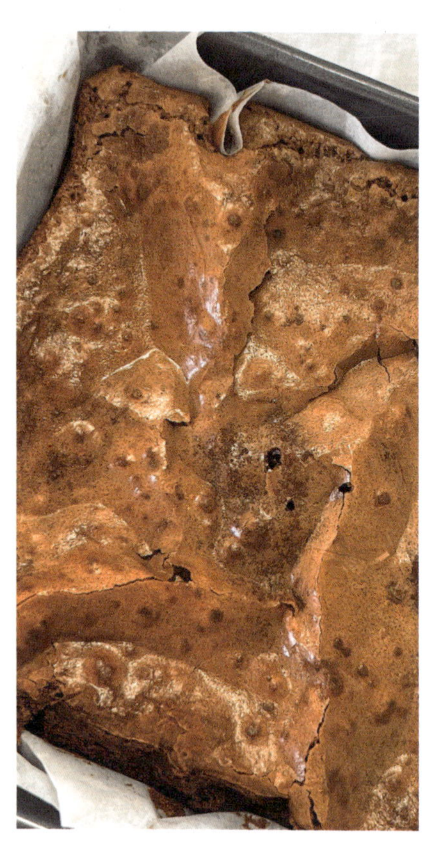

# Chocolate Brownies

*From my mother's recipe file, these brownies are fudgy with a crackly crust and often showed up in little squares at Sunday potlucks.*

**4 ounces (113g) semi-sweet or dark chocolate chips**
**½ cup (113g) unsalted butter**
**4 large eggs**
**2 cups (396g) white sugar**
**1 cup (120g) all-purpose flour**
**1 teaspoon (4.3g) pure vanilla extract**
**½ teaspoon (2.84g) sea salt**

In a medium bowl set over a pan of simmering hot water on the stovetop, melt the butter and the chocolate. (The bottom of the bowl should not touch the water.) Stir until smooth, then remove from the heat and cool. Add the eggs, one at a time, stirring well after each addition. Then, add the sugar and stir to incorporate, then add the flour and mix until blended. Lastly, stir in the vanilla and salt. Bake in a 9 x 9-inch baking pan lined with parchment paper. Bake at 325°F for 35 minutes. Cool, then cut into small squares.

*If using salted butter, omit adding salt in the recipe.*

# Rocky Road Bars

*Amish Community Cookbook*

*These bars are a cake-like brownie topped with an irresistible mixture of melted marshmallows, peanut butter and chocolate. During my years of teaching in an Amish School, parents sometimes brought these as a treat for the kids on days they provided a hot lunch for everyone.*

**1 cup (226g) butter**
**1½ cups (300g) white sugar**
**4 large eggs**
**2 teaspoons (8.6g) pure vanilla extract**
**½ teaspoon (2.84g) salt**
**½ teaspoon (2g) baking powder**
**¼ cup (21.25g) cocoa**
**1½ cups (180g) all-purpose flour**
**4 cups (200g) mini marshmallows**

**Top Layer**
**1½ cups (255g) chocolate chips**
**1½ cup (375g) peanut butter**
**2¼ cups (63g) Rice Krispies® cereal**

1. Beat butter and sugar until creamy. Add eggs and vanilla. Gradually add dry ingredients. Bake in a 9 x13-inch pan at 350°F for 15 minutes. Remove from oven. Sprinkle marshmallows on top and put back in oven. Bake until marshmallows are puffy. Allow to cool.

2. For the **Top Layer**, melt chocolate and peanut butter together. Stir in Rice Krispies. Spread over marshmallows. Cool before cutting.

# Raisin Top Cookies

*Esther Miller, Mt. Hope, Ohio*

*These old-fashioned cookies are topped with a delicious raisin filling and are similar to Thumbprint Cookies (page 125). My Aunt Elizabeth often kept these in her pantry.*

1 cup (213g) brown sugar
1 cup (200g) white sugar
1 cup (226g) butter
2 large eggs
1 tablespoon (13g) pure vanilla extract

¼ cup (61g) whole milk
4 cups (480g) all-purpose flour
1 teaspoon (5g) baking soda
¼ teaspoon (1.42g) sea salt

**Raisin Filling**

¾ cup (159.75g) brown sugar
1 cup (159g) raisins
1 cup (236.59g) water
¼ teaspoon (1.42g) sea salt

1. For the **Raisin Filling**: In a medium-sized pot, heat the sugar, raisins, water, and salt until it comes to boiling, for about 5 minutes, then thicken it with a slurry made from 1 tablespoon (7g) cornstarch mixed with ¼ cup (59.14g) water. Cook for an additional 5 minutes until filling starts to thicken. Add 1 teaspoon (4.3g) maple extract. Cool the filling before topping the cookies.

2. In the bowl of a stand mixer, cream the butter and sugar until fluffy, about 4 minutes. Add the eggs, one at a time, and beat until blended. Next add the vanilla and the milk. In a medium bowl, whisk together the flour, baking soda, and salt and add to the mixture. Whip until combined. Scoop the dough into balls and place on a parchment-lined cookie sheet. Make an indentation with your finger in each ball, and place 1 tablespoon of Raisin Filling in each. Bake at 350°F for about 12–14 minutes. Makes about 33 cookies.

# Amish Church Cookies

*Amish women sometimes make these cookies to take along to church services for their children to snack on. I grew up with these simple sugar cookies as a staple in our home. Years later, I added frosting to make them a little more special. Either way, they are easy and delicious.*

½ cup (113g) unsalted butter
1½ cups (150g) white sugar
2 large eggs, room temperature
1 cup (227g) sour cream, room temperature
1 teaspoon (5g) pure vanilla extract
1 tablespoon (15g) lemon juice
3 cups (360g) all-purpose flour
1 teaspoon (5.68g) sea salt
½ teaspoon (2g) baking powder
½ teaspoon (3g) baking soda

**Cinnamon Sugar**
¼ cup (25g) white sugar
½ teaspoon (1.4g) ground cinnamon

**Vanilla Frosting**
2 cups (452g) unsalted butter, room temperature
4 cups (480g) sifted confectioners' sugar
2 tablespoons (30.5g) milk
2 teaspoons (10g) pure vanilla extract
1 pinch sea salt

1. Measure and sift dry ingredients into a bowl and set aside. In the bowl of a stand mixer, cream the butter and sugar for several minutes on medium speed. Add eggs, one at a time, and mix until incorporated, then add sour cream, vanilla, and lemon juice. Mix on low speed and gradually add dry ingredients. Bake at 350°F for about 4 minutes on the bottom rack and 4 minutes on the top rack for a total of 8-10 minutes. (Don't overbake!) Cookies are done when they are dry on top and just barely turning golden around edges. Immediately dust with Cinnamon Sugar mixture or frost with Vanilla Frosting when cool.

2. For the **Vanilla Frosting**: In the bowl of a stand mixer, whip the butter until fluffy, about 5 minutes, then gradually add the confectioners' sugar, milk, vanilla, and sea salt. Beat for an additional 1 or 2 minutes, scraping the bowl during the process.

# Peanut Butter Chocolate Kiss Cookies

*A favorite of my children for years, we usually bake these cookies around the Christmas holiday season. They are a chewy little peanut butter sugar cookie with a Hershey's Kiss® nestled on top. These bake best if the dough has time to chill in the refrigerator for at least 2 hours prior to baking.*

- **½ cup (99g) white sugar**
- **½ cup (106.5g) brown sugar**
- **½ cup (113g) butter, softened**
- **½ cup (125g) Jif® peanut butter (natural peanut butter does not work well in this recipe)**
- **1 large egg**
- **2 tablespoons (30.4g) whole milk**
- **1 teaspoon (4.3g) pure vanilla extract**
- **1¾ cups (210g) all-purpose flour**
- **1 teaspoon (6g) baking soda**
- **½ teaspoon (3g) sea salt**
- **1 bag (17.9 ounces [507.45g]) Hershey's Chocolate Kisses**
- **1 additional cup (200g) of white sugar to roll the cookies**

Cream sugars, butter, and peanut butter together in the bowl of a stand mixer for about 5 minutes until fluffy. Beat in the eggs, one at a time, then add milk and vanilla. In a medium-sized mixing bowl, whisk together the flour, baking soda, and salt. Add to the peanut butter mixture and combine thoroughly, scraping the bowl. Chill the dough in the refrigerator for at least 2 hours or overnight, then scoop into balls using a small (2 tablespoons) cookie scoop. Roll each ball in a bowl of white sugar, then place on cookie sheets lined with parchment paper. Working with one tray at a time, bake at 350°F for 5 minutes, then rotate the pan and bake for an additional 4 minutes. Remove from the oven and press 1 kiss into each cookie, then return to the oven and bake for an additional 2–3 minutes. Yields 24 cookies

# Chocolate Peanut Butter Rice Krispies Bars

*Gooey and rich with chocolate and peanut butter, these bars are great to serve at parties and holiday events.*

8 cups (224g) Rice Krispies cereal
½ teaspoon (2.84g) coarse Kosher salt*
7 cups (391g) mini marshmallows
½ cup (113g) unsalted butter
¼ cup (64.5g) natural peanut butter
½ teaspoon (2.15g) maple extract
8 ounces (226.8g) semi-sweet chocolate chips
½ cup (120g) heavy cream
½ tablespoon (7.5g) maple syrup

*It's important to use coarse salt and not fine salt in this recipe, or they will be too salty.*

1. In a medium-sized mixing bowl, measure out the Rice Krispies and the salt. In a large heavy bottom pot, melt the butter until it starts to foam, then add the marshmallows and stir constantly until melted. Add the peanut butter and stir to combine, then pour over the bowl of Rice Krispies and stir gently until blended. Pour into a 9 x 9-inch baking pan buttered and lined with parchment paper. Press down gently until even. Set aside to cool.

2. In a small saucepan, heat the heavy cream until it starts to boil. Pour over the chocolate chips in a bowl, set in a cozy spot, and cover. Let it set for about 5–8 minutes, then whisk briskly until smooth. Add the maple syrup and stir to combine, then pour over the Rice Krispies. Let it rest until the chocolate is firm, then cut into bars and serve. Store in an airtight container on the counter.

# Christmas Cookies

*Mary Miller, Mt. Hope, Ohio*

*Mary is a sweet Amish lady who cleaned our house and helped to take care of our children when they were little. She always made these cookies for them at Christmas, and they have been a favorite ever since.*

1½ cups (297g) white sugar
1 cup (226g) butter or shortening, at room temperature
2 large eggs
4 cups (480g) all-purpose flour
2 teaspoons (8g) baking powder
2 teaspoons (8g) cream of tartar
2 teaspoons (8g) baking soda
¾ cup (183.g) whole milk
½ tablespoon (7.5g) lemon juice

**Frosting**

6 tablespoons (85g) butter
3½ cups (420g) confectioners' sugar
4 tablespoons (60.92g) milk
2 teaspoons (8.4g) pure vanilla extract

In the bowl of a stand mixer, beat the sugar and the butter or shortening for about 2 minutes. Add the eggs, one at a time, and beat until blended, about 1 minute. Whisk together the dry ingredients and add them alternately with the milk and lemon juice. Chill dough for several hours before trying to roll it out. Roll out dough on a floured counter top to about ⅛–¼ inch thick. Cut out shapes with your favorite cookie cutters. Re-roll dough with leftover scraps, repeating until all the dough is used up. Bake at 325°F for about 5–7 minutes, depending on how thick you roll out the dough. Don't overbake. Top each cookie with Frosting. Yield varies depending on the size of the cookie cutters used, at least 30–40 cookies.

# Oatmeal Raisin Cookies

*Esther Miller, Mt. Hope, Ohio*

*Warmly spiced, these cookies are studded with plump raisins and chewy oats.*

- 1 cup (240g) water
- 2 cups (400g) raisins
- 1 cup (190g) shortening or butter
- 2 cups (400g) white sugar
- 2 large eggs
- 1 teaspoon (4.34g) pure vanilla extract
- 2¼ cups (270g) all-purpose flour
- 2 cups (198g) oats
- 1 teaspoon (4.8g) baking powder
- 1 teaspoon (5.6g) baking soda
- 1½ teaspoons (8.64g) sea salt
- 1½ teaspoons (3.9g) ground cinnamon
- ½ teaspoon (1g) ground nutmeg
- ¼ teaspoon (0.5g) ground allspice

Boil raisins in water for 5 minutes; drain and cool. In the bowl of a stand mixer, cream the sugar and shortening or butter for about 5 minutes until light and fluffy. Add the eggs, one at a time, and beat just until blended in, then add vanilla extract and the cooled raisins. Whisk dry ingredients together and blend in slowly, mixing until just barely incorporated. Scoop onto cookie sheets lined with parchment paper and bake at 375°F for about 10–12 minutes. Cookies should not be brown when pulled from the oven. Yields 16–20 cookies.

# Chocolate Chip Cookies

*A favorite with my kids for many years, these classic chocolate chip cookies are made with dark chocolate chips and finished off with a sprinkle of flake sea salt on top. They are great for dunking in hot chocolate!*

- 1⅓ cups (301.33g) unsalted butter
- 1 cup (200g) white sugar
- 1 cup (213g) brown sugar
- 2 large eggs
- 3⅓ cups (400g) all-purpose flour
- 1 teaspoon (6g) baking soda
- 1 teaspoon (5.69g) salt
- 2 teaspoons (8.6g) pure vanilla extract
- 1½ cups (255g) dark chocolate chips (70% dark chocolate)
- Maldon flake sea salt, for sprinkling

In the bowl of a stand mixer, beat the butter and sugars together until creamy, about 5 minutes. Add the eggs, one a time, scraping the bowl and beating just to incorporate. In a small bowl, whisk together the flour, baking soda, and salt, then add to the mixer and blend to incorporate. Fold in the chocolate chips. Scrape the bowl thoroughly, to make sure no butter is hanging out in the bottom of the mixer bowl. Scoop onto parchment-lined baking sheets. Bake at 350°F. I use a 3-inch cookie scoop and bake them for about 5-6 minutes on the lower oven rack and then 5-6 minutes on the middle oven rack. Smaller cookies will bake for less time. Pull them out of the oven when they are just turning golden around the edges and the tops are almost dry. Allow them to rest on the baking tray for 10 minutes before moving to a cooling rack. Sprinkle with flake salt, if desired. Yields 16–20 cookies.

# Lemon Curd Squares

*Baked in a shortbread crust and topped with a luscious lemon filling, these classic-style lemon bars are a tart treat for afternoon tea.*

**Crust**
1 cup (226g) butter, room temperature
½ cup (56.75g) confectioners' sugar
2½ cups (300g) all-purpose flour
1 teaspoon (5.68g) sea salt

**Lemon FIlling**
2 cups (200g) white sugar
1 teaspoon (4g) baking powder
½ cup (60g) all-purpose flour
¼ cup (56.5g) butter, melted
1 cup (244g) lemon juice
1 tablespoon (6g) lemon zest

1. For the **Crust**: In a mixer bowl, beat the butter and sugar together, then add in the flour and salt and beat until crumbly and blended. Press evenly into a 9 x 12-inch baking dish. Bake at 350°F for 20 minutes, then remove from oven and immediately top with filling.

2. To make the **Lemon Filling**: Beat eggs until frothy. Whisk the sugar, flour, and baking soda in a bowl, then add gradually to the eggs and beat until blended. Slowly add the melted butter, lemon juice, and zest. Beat until all blended, scraping bowl. Pour the filling gently over the baked crust and bake for an additional 25 minutes until the filling is set. Cool completely, then cut into squares. Before serving, dust with confectioners' sugar.

COOKIES, BROWNIES & BARS

# Peanut Butter Chocolate Chip Bars

*Ruth Mast, Zanesville, Ohio*

*Sometimes referred to as chipper bars, these soft and chewy bars are often seen at church potlucks or reunions. The trick is to not overbake them, so they stay a bit gooey.*

2 cups (198g) oats
1 cup (120g) all-purpose flour
1 cup (165g) brown sugar
½ teaspoon (3g) baking soda
½ teaspoon (2.84g) sea salt
¾ cup (169.5g) butter, melted
14 ounces (396g) sweetened condensed milk
⅓ cup (90g) peanut butter
1 cup (170g) chocolate chips, to sprinkle on top

In a medium bowl, whisk together the oats, flour, sugar, baking soda, and salt, then add the melted butter and mix until crumbly. Reserve 1½ cups of the mixture. Press the remaining crumbs into the bottom of a greased 9 x 13-inch pan. In a small bowl, stir together the sweetened condensed milk and the peanut butter. Pour this mixture evenly over the crumb mixture in the pan. Pat the reserved crumb mixture into the filling and sprinkle with chocolate chips. Bake at 350°F for 25–30 minutes, or until light brown. Remove from the oven when the bars are still jiggly.

# Buttermilk Brownies

*Amish Community Cookbook*

*Similar to Texas sheet cake, these brownies are made with buttermilk and then covered in a warm chocolate frosting that melts into a shiny glaze.*

1 cup (226g) butter
3 tablespoons (15.94g) cocoa powder
1 cup (236.59g) water
2 cups (200g) white sugar
2 large eggs, fork beaten
½ cup (112g) whole-fat buttermilk
1 teaspoon (5g) pure vanilla extract
½ teaspoon (2.84g) sea salt
1 teaspoon (6g) baking soda
2 cups (240g) all-purpose flour

**Chocolate Buttermilk Frosting**

¼ cup (56.5g) butter
3 tablespoons (15.94g) cocoa powder
3 tablespoons (42g) whole-fat buttermilk
2 cups (330g) confectioners' sugar, sifted
1 teaspoon (5g) pure vanilla extract

1. In a medium saucepan, combine the butter, cocoa powder, water, and sugar. Bring to a boil, whisking constantly. Remove from heat and pour into the bowl of a stand mixer. In a small bowl, combine the eggs, buttermilk, and vanilla, whisking until smooth. In another bowl, whisk together the flour, baking soda, and salt. With the mixer on low speed, gradually drizzle in the buttermilk mixture, then slowly add the flour mixture. Scrape the bowl periodically and mix until well blended.

2. Lightly butter a 10 x 15-inch jelly roll pan or line it with parchment paper. Pour the batter into the pan and bake at 350°F for about 20-25 minutes. Brownies are done when the top starts to crack slightly, and a toothpick inserted comes out a bit gooey. Remove from oven and prepare the Chocolate Buttermilk Frosting.

3. To make the **Chocolate Buttermilk Frosting**, melt the butter, cocoa powder, and buttermilk together in a saucepan. Whisk to blend well. Place into the bowl of a stand mixer and beat in confectioners' sugar and vanilla. Spread over brownies while they are still warm.

# Sea Foam Squares

*Geneva Schlabach, Sarasota, Florida*

*These old-school bars have a cookie base with a chocolate filling and are covered in a crackly meringue topping. Using a dark chocolate instead of semi-sweet or milk chocolate chips helps to temper the sweetness of these bars.*

- 1⅛ cups (213.75g) Crisco
- ¾ cup (150g) white sugar
- ¾ cup (123.75g) brown sugar
- 4 large egg yolks (save the whites for meringue portion)
- 1½ tablespoons (22.18g) water
- 1½ teaspoons (7.5g) pure vanilla extract
- 3 cups (360g) all-purpose flour
- ½ teaspoon (2.84g) sea salt
- ½ teaspoon (3g) baking soda
- 1½ teaspoons (7g) baking powder
- 1½ cups (255g) dark chocolate chips

**Meringue Topping**

- 4 large egg whites
- 2 cups (330g) brown sugar

1. In a mixer bowl, cream together the shortening and sugar until fluffy. Scrape the bowl, then add the egg yolks, water, and vanilla and beat again until blended. Scrape the bowl. In a separate bowl, stir together the flour, salt, baking soda and baking powder. Add dry ingredients to the mixer bowl and beat all together until blended. Spread this mixture onto a cookie sheet (16½ x 12 inches) and press firmly into base of pan. Over this, sprinkle the chocolate chips and press them into the dough.

2. For the **Meringue Topping**, beat the egg whites until they have soft peaks. Add the brown sugar and beat until you have stiff peaks. Spread this mixture over the cookie dough, taking it almost to the edge of the pan. Bake at 350°F for 15–20 minutes. When the edge of the cookie crust is just turning golden, the bars are done. Do not overbake. Cool slightly, then cut into squares and serve. Yields approximately 24 bars.

# Chocolate Sorghum Sugar Cookies

*The rich taste of sorghum mixed with spices and chocolate gives these soft and chewy sugar cookies their appeal.*

**½ cup (99g) raw cane sugar**
**½ cup (82.5g) brown sugar**
**¾ cup (169.5g) butter, at room temperature**
**1 large egg**
**4 tablespoons (84g) sorghum syrup**
**2 teaspoons (10g) pure vanilla extract**
**1 teaspoon (2.8g) ground cinnamon**
**½ teaspoon (2.84g) sea salt**
**2 teaspoons (3.52g) ground ginger**
**1½ teaspoons (9g) baking soda**
**2 cups (240g) all-purpose flour**
**½ cup (58g) cocoa powder**
**White sugar to roll the cookies**

In the bowl of a stand mixer, beat the sugar and butter until blended, then add the egg, sorghum, and vanilla and beat until blended, scraping the bowl several times. In a separate bowl, whisk the cinnamon, salt, ginger, baking soda, and flour, then add this to the first mixture and blend. Dough will be very firm. Scoop cookies with a small scoop, roll in sugar, and then roll between your palms. Place on a parchment-lined cookie sheet and flatten slightly with the bottom of a glass or spatula. Bake at 350°F for a total of about 6–8 minutes. Don't overbake! They are done when they start to crack. They will be soft when you remove them from the oven, but they will firm up after they sit for a few minutes. You want the texture to be almost cake-like, not crunchy. Yields 16–20 cookies.

# Chocolate Oat Bars

*The star of this oatmeal bar is the irresistible swirl of chocolate mixed with Eagle Brand condensed milk and butter. They are perfect for packing in lunches, taking on a picnic, or to eat for an afternoon snack.*

- 3 cups (297g) organic oats
- 2½ cups (300g) all-purpose flour
- 1 teaspoon (6g) baking soda
- ½ teaspoon (2.84g) sea salt
- 1 cup (226g) unsalted butter
- 2 cups (330g) brown sugar
- 2 large eggs
- 2 teaspoons (8.68g) pure vanilla extract

**Chocolate Mixture**

- One 14-ounce (396g) can Eagle Brand sweetened condensed milk
- 1½ cups (255g) semi-sweet or milk chocolate chips
- ½ teaspoon (2.84g) sea salt
- 2 tablespoons (28.4g) unsalted butter
- 2 teaspoons (8.68g) pure vanilla extract

1. Combine oats, flour, baking soda, and salt, and whisk together. Set aside. Beat the butter for about a minute and then add the sugar and beat for about 4 minutes until fluffy. Add the eggs, one at a time, and then the vanilla. Beat until well combined. Pat two-thirds of the oat mixture into the bottom of an ungreased 9 x 13-inch pan. (It will be sticky. Using a spatula or a butter knife helps.) Spread the Chocolate Mixture over the dough. Dot the remaining oat mixture over the Chocolate Mixture. Bake at 350°F for about 25 minutes. Cool, and cut into bars to serve. These bars are best when they are not overbaked.

2. For the **Chocolate Mixture**, heat together the milk, chocolate, butter, and salt over low heat, stirring until smooth. Remove from heat and stir in the vanilla.

# Thumbprint Cookies

*Esther Miller, Mt. Hope, Ohio*

*Topped with a dollop of jam, these cookies are great for holidays or special occasions.*

**2 cups (426g) brown sugar**
**1 cup (226g) unsalted butter, room temperature**
**2 large eggs**
**4 cups (480g) all-purpose flour**
**1 teaspoon (6g) baking soda**
**½ teaspoon sea salt**
**4 tablespoons (61g) milk**
**1 tablespoon (15g) vanilla extract**

1. In the bowl of a stand mixer, beat the softened butter with the sugar for several minutes until fluffy. Add the eggs, one at a time, blending until incorporated. Whisk together the flour, baking soda, and salt, then add to the bowl, along with the milk and vanilla extract. Beat until incorporated, scraping the bowl.

2. Roll the dough into walnut-sized balls (approximately 1½ inches in diameter). Place on parchment-lined cookie sheet and, with your thumb, make a hole in the middle of each one for the filling. Fill the hole with jam or preserves. Bake at 350°F for about 8 minutes. Yields 36 cookies.

# Monster Cookies

*These have been the most requested cookies in my home since the kids were little, and now the grandchildren ask for them, too. Made with oats instead of flour, they are chewy and delicious if they are not overbaked.*

**¾ cup (169.5g) butter, room temperature**
**1 cup (200g) white sugar**
**1 cup (213g) brown sugar**
**4 large eggs**
**2 cups (540g) peanut butter**
**½ tablespoon (8.53g) sea salt**
**5 cups (495g) organic oats**
**1 cup (200g) M&M's® candies**
**2 cups (340g) milk chocolate chips**

In the bowl of a stand mixer, cream together the butter and sugar for about 4 minutes, until fluffy. Scrape the bowl. Beat in the eggs, one at a time, and then add the peanut butter and just until blended. Next, add the oats, M&M's, and chocolate chips and stir until blended. Scoop onto cookie sheets lined with parchment paper and bake at 325°F for about 10 minutes. Cookies are done when they are just turning brown around the edges but still look a little undone in the middle. They will set up after they are removed from the oven. Garnish with flake sea salt, if desired. Yields 16–20 cookies.

# The Black Stockings

*Each sect of the Amish has their own set of rules called the* Ordnung. *Women must wear bonnets, full-length, modest dresses with capes on the shoulders, shawls, black shoes, and stockings. They do so to reflect their reluctance to change, respect for tradition, and their biblical interpretation against conforming to the ways of the "English" world. The bishop of each sect gets to decide what type of stockings the women will wear. By not following the rules of attire, a woman can be shunned from their church and family.*

The black stockings were the straw that broke the camel's back. I was sitting in church one night as a teenager, listening to the bishop go over the rules of our Conservative Mennonite congregation. There was a long list: plain dresses and head coverings required, no wearing of gold or jewelry, no television or radios permitted. My mind shifted to neutral because I had heard these things so many times before. But then I heard, "And we will no longer tolerate flesh-colored stockings (hosiery). Black stockings must be worn at all times."

My future flashed before me in a long, unbroken drudge of rules. I walked out of that service and within a few days away from the Mennonite church. Looking back, that was the hardest thing I ever did. It was hard because my father was that Bishop. I can still see the disbelief in his eyes when I told him I no longer wanted to be part of the Mennonites.

Thankfully, my parents didn't shun me, which is more typical of Amish churches. And as they grew older in years, they became more accepting of the path I chose. My husband and I raised our kids on the family farm and spent many happy years living across the street from them. Even though that was a hard decision to make, I'm grateful I had the courage to do it. While I'm deeply respectful of my heritage and have maintained many of its values, God led me to follow a path that was uniquely right for me.

These are the typical socks that Amish women wear.

# Communion and Foot Washing

*Communion and foot washing are very significant religious practices for the Amish. They represent humility, reconciliation, and community. Communion, the passing of bread and wine, is a symbolic reference to the body and blood of Christ. In the Amish community, communion happens twice per year. Foot washing also only takes place during communion. It follows the footsteps of Jesus, who washed his disciples' feet before he was betrayed. This practice represents humility and service.*

Twice a year, our Conservative Mennonite church had a service where all the members who were obedient to the church's standards participated in the sacrament of Holy Communion. To determine whether one could join in this holy tradition required an interview process with the bishop and ministers of the church in a private room. My first communion took place at the age of 16, after I was baptized. I remember going into a room with four ministers and my father, who was the bishop, and answering the question, "Are you in obedience to the church's standards of discipline, and are you at peace with God and your fellow man?"

After a trepidatious "Yes," and if there were no rumors of me having worn flesh-colored stockings or having attended a move theater, I received the confirmation I could participate in communion the following Sunday. For those not so lucky, they were given a chance to repent for their misdeeds. If unwilling, they were forbidden to join in Communion with the rest of the congregation. Generally, two missed communions resulted in potential excommunication from the church.

The Communion service was a long affair, which involved listening to several sermons followed by acapella singing of the congregation, while ministers passed a cup of grape juice to each person, who took a sip and passed it to the person beside them. Then came the plate of bread, which was torn into small pieces and given to each person by another minister. Afterwards came the foot-washing ceremony with men and women going into separate rooms and taking turns to sit down and wash each other's feet in accordance with Jesus's command in John 13:14.

This was a solemn affair, with the singing of hymns throughout and a general feeling of relief after the last foot had been washed and we could finally go home to Sunday lunch.

# The Covering

*Women must wear a prayer covering or a bonnet once they are baptized in the Amish faith. The coverings are worn for many reasons: modesty, practicality, and identity. Many sects have their own type of covering so that they will be recognized as a part of that sect.*

Amish and Mennonite women wear the traditional head covering according to what they believe the Bible states in 1 Corinthians 11:5, which says, "And every woman who prays or prophesies with her head uncovered dishonors her head—it is just as though her head were shaved." While sizes and shapes vary across denominations and churches, with Mennonites becoming less likely to wear them, the covering is one of the defining symbols of the plain people.

My mother was a seamstress who sewed coverings for Mennonite women, not only in our state, but in others. She would sit at her sewing machine, happily singing a tune while tucking tiny pleats into a cap made of a white net material. Nearby, stacks of completed coverings in various sizes were waiting to be packaged for shipping, or for someone who stopped by to purchase one.

I wore my hair in braids until around the age of 10 when I started wearing my first covering. I never thought to question it for many years, accepting it as a way of life. It was one of the things I gladly relinquished when leaving the Mennonite church.

This is my niece, Ruth Rabatin, modeling the Mennonite-style covering she wears on a daily basis. Ruth and her daughters make these coverings on a sewing machine in their sunny kitchen.

While many Amish women make their own coverings, some local stores may carry them—though availability can vary from place to place.

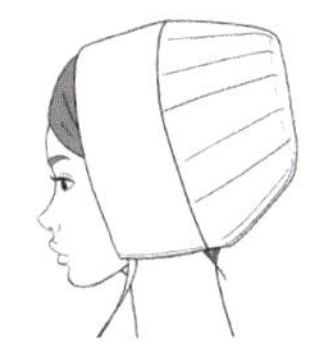

A white covering worn by many Amish girls while working.

The Amish bonnet serves as more than just a traditional head covering—it is a powerful symbol of faith, modesty, and cultural identity. Its color often conveys marital status, with white typically worn by married women and black by those who are unmarried. Variations in bonnet style and material reflect seasonal changes, religious occasions, and differences among Amish orders, blending functionality with deep cultural meaning. Above all, the bonnet reflects the community's commitment to simplicity and its conscious separation from modern influences.

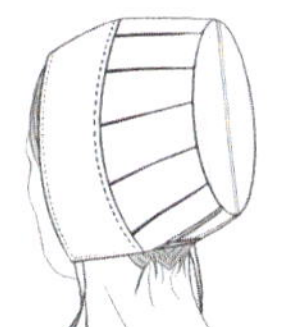

Old Order Amish, Holmes County, OH.

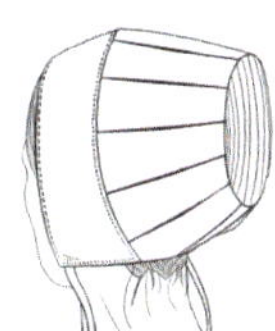

New Order Amish, Holmes County, OH.

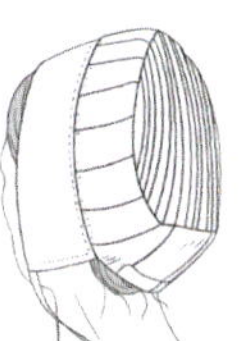

Andy Weaver Amish.

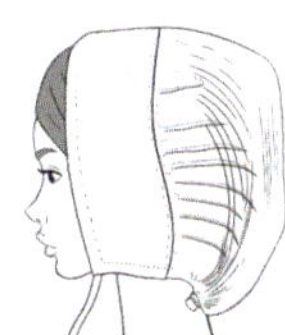

Swartzentruber Amish.

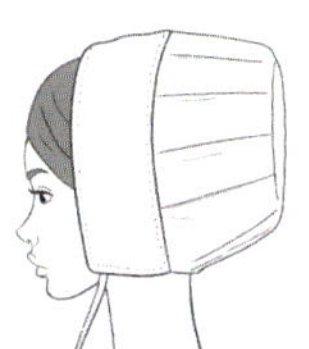

New Amish Settlements in Ohio.

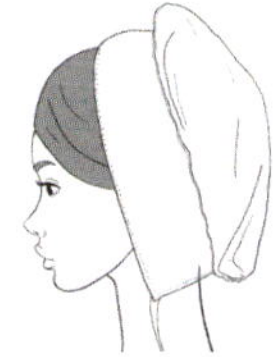

Geauga County Amish.

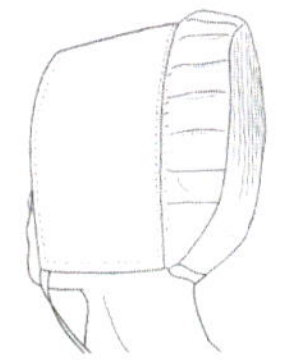

Lancaster County, Pennsylvania Amish.

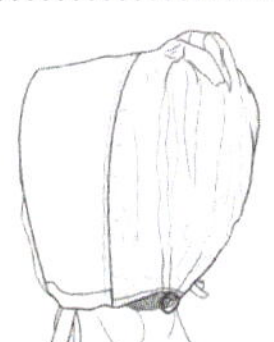

Nebraska Amish.

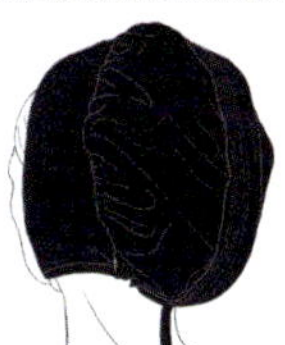

Black bonnet of the Amish in Milverton, Ontario.

A heavier-material black bonnet of the Amish in Milverton, Ontario.

A veiling worn by Amish and Mennonite women when doing tasks.

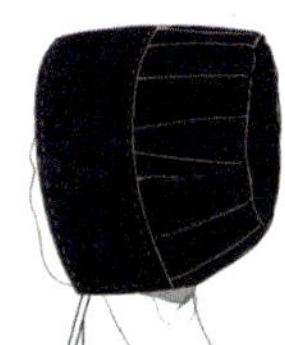

A black bonnet covering worn by unmarried Amish girls to church.

# CHAPTER 5

I was never far from my mother on bread-baking day. Her patience was infinite, and she never failed to let me help her. I wonder if she thought, all those years ago when she taught my small hands how to shape the dough, that one day I would be teaching others the same process and telling stories of how she taught me most everything I know in the kitchen.

"Smack it just so," Mother would say as my clumsy fingers handled the dough, trying to shape the loaves as she did. And then I pricked the loaves with a fork and lined up the pans on the kitchen counter while we waited for the bread to rise. Soon enough it was time for those loaves to go into the oven. How good the kitchen smelled when all the bread was baking! She always made enough for our family, and anyone else who happened along right at the time that bread came out of the oven. I would think the neighbors smelled the bread and timed their appearance at the front door. But she didn't mind. It always made her happy to share the labor of her hands.

When the bread came out of the oven, it was my job to brush the tops with melted butter. Oh, how I loved that glow! And, of course, it was my job to cut into a warm loaf and slather a thick slice with that same melted butter and top it with Mother's strawberry jam. It was the best thing in the world for a kid's hungry belly.

My mother started baking Honey Wheat Bread (page 139) in 1940 when she married my father. Decades later when I was born, this bread was still showing up at the table for every meal. Throughout the years of raising my own family, Mother kept this bread coming to our table as well, delivering still-warm loaves, which we sliced and ate with butter and honey. When she passed on, I continued the tradition of baking her bread from the time-worn recipe written in her delicate script. When we started our bakery in 2017, this bread came along as a beautiful representation of everything my mother was to me: comfort, warmth, gentleness, and filled with so much goodness.

## • RECIPES •

Me at age 18, carrying on the tradition of baking bread just like my mother.

My mother, Esther Stutzman, baking bread in her kitchen in 1974.

# Bread

BREAD

# How to Make Pumpkin Dinner Rolls

*Esther Miller, Mt. Hope, Ohio*

*Even though we had homemade bread every day, my mother didn't bake dinner rolls often. But when she did, it was a special occasion such as Thanksgiving or Christmas. They can seem intimidating to make, but they are really not. It helps if you can make them alongside someone who has done it before, so here is a step-by-step process you can follow.*

## Ingredients

2 packages (4½ teaspoons, 13.5g) yeast
1 cup (244g) warm milk
1 cup (245g) pumpkin puree
2 large eggs
⅓ cup (75.33g) salted butter, melted
½ cup (100g) white sugar
1½ teaspoons (8.53g) sea salt
5½ to 6 cups (660–720g) all-purpose flour

**1. Prepare the dough.** The first thing we will do is activate the yeast by placing it in the warm milk (test it with your finger to make sure the milk is not too hot). I like to use a 2-cup Pyrex liquid measuring cup and, after the yeast has been added to the liquid, I cover it with a cloth to keep it cozy while I mix up the rest of the ingredients. While the yeast is resting, put the pumpkin puree, eggs, melted butter, sugar and salt into the bowl of a stand mixer. With the paddle attachment, mix everything together until blended. Switch to the dough hook and slowly add the flour. I like to stop at 5 cups of flour to assess how the dough looks. If it's still sticky, keep adding flour, ½ cup at a time, until the dough is soft but does not stick to your hands. The dough will pull away from the sides of the bowl when it is done. Remove the dough from the bowl, shape it into a round, and put it into a medium-sized mixing bowl that has been buttered lightly. Cover with a cloth and let it rise for 1 hour or until it doubles in size.

**2.** While the dough is rising, butter a 9 x 13-inch pan for baking.

**3.** When the dough has doubled in size, make a fist with your hand and gently punch down the dough all around, deflating the rise.

**4.** Sprinkle a little flour onto the counter, gather the dough out of the bowl, and place it on the counter, forming it into a ball.

**5.** With a sharp knife, divide the dough into equal halves.

**6.** Form the dough into 2 logs. Take each half of dough and gently roll it back and forth across the counter, forming it into 2 logs of equal length, approximately 12 inches long.

7. With a sharp knife, score the dough logs evenly into 6 pieces each, then cut them.

8. Working with one piece at a time, take a piece of dough and roll it into a ball. Do this by cupping your hand firmly over it and working it around in short movements. This works best on a counter that doesn't have flour on it. When it has been shaped into a ball, place it in a buttered 9 x 13-inch baking pan. Do this until all the rolls have been shaped.

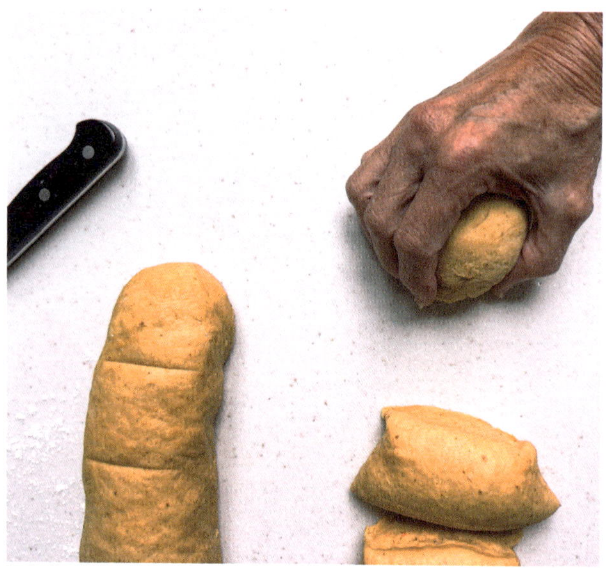

9. Cover the rolls with a cloth and let them rise for 20-30 minutes while you preheat the oven to 350°F.

10. Bake the rolls for about 20 minutes or until golden brown. They will be puffy and start to pull apart when they are done. Remove them from the oven and brush them with melted butter.

**11. Eat them!** This is the best part of making dinner rolls! If your family is lucky enough to come into the kitchen as you are pulling them out of the oven, all you need to do is set out some butter and jelly and everyone will be happy.

*The pumpkin in this recipe is not for taste, but for texture. It keeps the rolls soft. If you want a pumpkin taste, just add some cinnamon or pumpkin pie spice. Also, these make 12 large rolls. If you would like them smaller, simply divide the dough into 4 pieces instead of 2 and then roll into 4 logs and cut each log into 6 pieces to make 24 rolls.*

# Dinner Buns

*These soft and fluffy buns were often served for Sunday lunch alongside mashed potatoes and gravy, meatloaf, and Amish noodles. Refrigerating the dough overnight, working out the dough into pans the next morning, and allowing the buns to rise for several hours while parishioners went to church meant the buns could be popped into the oven directly after the service. The buns were eaten warm with butter and jelly.*

- ¼ cup (59.15g) warm water
- 1 teaspoon (4.13g) plus ½ cup (100g) white sugar, divided
- 4½ teaspoons (14g) dry active yeast
- 1 tablespoon (15g) sea salt
- ¼ cup (56.5g) salted butter, melted
- 2 cups (473.18g) hot tap water
- 2 large eggs, beaten
- 7 cups (840g) all-purpose flour

1. Stir the warm water, 1 teaspoon white sugar, and the dry active yeast together briefly and allow to rest in a warm place until the yeast has activated, about 5 minutes.

2. In a large mixing bowl, stir together the sea salt, butter, ½ cup of white sugar, and tap water until sugar has dissolved. Then, add the yeast mixture.

3. Add the beaten eggs and 4 cups of flour into the bowl of ingredients from steps 1 and 2. Stir to combine. Then, add 3 additional cups of flour and stir until blended. Cover the bowl tightly with plastic wrap and place in the refrigerator overnight. About 3.5 hours before you are ready to serve them, remove the dough from the refrigerator and divide it into 4 equal portions.

4. On a floured countertop, roll each portion into a log and slice into about 7 equal portions. Then, roll each portion into a bun and place in a buttered pan, nestling together about 6 per pan. Let them rise for about 2 hours or until double in size and then bake at 350°F for approximately 20 minutes. Brush with melted butter when you remove them from the oven. Makes 30 buns.

**Note:** Dough may be kept in refrigerator for up to 2 days.

# Christmas Bread

*Amish Community Cookbook*

*For all the maraschino cherry lovers, this one is for you. Packed with coconut, bananas, oranges, dates, and cherries, this sweet bread looks festive on your holiday table.*

- ½ cup (113g) butter
- 1 cup (200g) sugar
- 2 large eggs
- 1 teaspoon (4.3g) pure vanilla extract
- 1 teaspoon (6g) baking soda
- ½ teaspoon (2.84g) salt
- 2 cups (240g) all-purpose flour
- 1 cup (225g) mashed bananas
- 1 cup (189g) mandarin oranges, drained
- 1 cup (100g) shredded coconut
- 1 cup (170g) milk or semi-sweet chocolate chips
- ⅔ cup (73.2g) sliced almonds divided
- ½ cup (77.5g) maraschino cherries, chopped
- ½ cup (112.50g) dates, chopped

In the bowl of a stand mixer, beat the butter and sugar until creamy. Add the eggs and vanilla and beat well. Whisk together the flour, salt, and baking soda and add to the butter mixture alternately with the mashed bananas. Stir in the remaining ingredients using only half the almonds. Spoon into one large loaf pan (9.5 x 5.5 inches) that has been buttered and floured or lined with parchment paper. Sprinkle almonds on top. Bake at 350°F for 45 minutes, then reduce heat to 325°F and continue baking (up to 1 hour) until a toothpick inserted in center comes out clean.

# Oatmeal Bread

*Wholesome and soft, this bread is made with organic old-fashioned oats, all-purpose flour, and sorghum. It is delicious for toast!*

- 1¼ cup (354.88g) boiling water
- 1 cup (90g) organic old-fashioned oats
- 2 packets (7g) active dry yeast, dissolved in ½ cup (118.29g) warm water
- ½ cup (170g) sorghum or molasses
- 1 tablespoon (17.06g) sea salt
- ⅓ cup (68.53g) oil
- 6 cups (750.93g) all-purpose flour, divided

Pour the boiling water over the oats in a small mixing bowl and cover. Let it rest. Meanwhile, place the yeast in ½ cup warm water and cover. Let the oats and the yeast mixture rest for about 5–8 minutes. In the bowl of a stand mixer, mix the sorghum, salt, oil, oats mixture, and 1 cup flour, then add the yeast mixture and an additional 5 cups of flour. Mix until it starts to pull away from the side of the bowl. If dough is still tacky, add an extra ½ cup (60g) flour and mix for a few minutes. Place dough in a buttered mixing bowl and cover with a cloth. Let it rise in a warm place until double in size, approximately 1 hour. Punch down the dough, divide in half, and shape into 2 loaves. Place in buttered loaf pans and allow to rise again for approximately 30 minutes, until dough has risen above the pans and has doubled in size. Bake at 350°F for 30–40 minutes until nicely browned and bottom of loaf sounds hollow when tapped. Remove from pans, brush with butter, and cool completely.

# Pluckets

*An old recipe for pull-apart sweet buns, these bake in an angel food pan and are delicious when served warm fresh from the oven.*

**2½ teaspoons (8.75g) yeast**
**¼ cup (59.15g) warm water**
**1 cup (244g) milk**
**⅓ cup (66g) white sugar**
**⅓ cup (75.33) butter**
**1½ teaspoons (5.69g) salt**
**3 large eggs, beaten slightly**
**4–5 cups (480g–600g) all-purpose flour**

**Butter/Sugar Mixture**

**½ cup (113g) butter, melted**
**1½ cup (297g) white sugar**
**4 teaspoons (10.4g) ground cinnamon**

1. Dissolve the yeast in the warm water and set aside for 5 minutes. Meanwhile, in a small saucepan, warm the milk, sugar, butter, and salt on stovetop. Remove from heat and when lukewarm, pour into the bowl of a stand mixer. Add the beaten eggs, flour, and yeast water and mix until dough starts pulling away from sides of the bowl. Add more flour as needed to make a stiff dough. Cover and let rise until double for about 1 hour. Knead down and let rise again. Punch down the dough and then form it into small balls about the size of walnuts (in their shell).

2. Combine the sugar and cinnamon. Dip each dough ball in melted butter, then roll in the cinnamon-sugar mixture. Pile balls loosely in an ungreased angel food pan and let them rise for 30 minutes. Bake them for 10 minutes at 400°F and then for 30 minutes at 350°F.

3. Remove from pan immediately. The buns will be stuck together, and that's how you serve them. Everyone plucks a bun from the central supply.

*It's a good idea to place the angel food cake pan with pluckets on a baking tray to bake, so the tray will catch the butter spilling over the top as the rolls puff up during the baking process.*

# Nathan's Cornbread

*Ruth Mast, Hopewell, Ohio*

*This recipe is from my sister, whose oldest son, Nathan, and his family live in the Dominican Republic where they have been Mennonite missionaries for many years. The cornbread is delicious when served warm with honey and butter.*

**2 cups (312g) corn meal**
**2 cups (240g) all-purpose flour**
**½ cup ((106.5g) brown sugar, packed**
**8 teaspoons (32g) baking powder**
**1 teaspoon (5.69g) sea salt**
**2 cups (488g) whole milk**
**4 large eggs**
**½ cup (108.59g) oil**
**Cinnamon, for topping**

Whisk dry ingredients together in a bowl. Then, mix in the eggs, milk, and oil, and stir until blended. Pour into a buttered 9 x 13-inch pan and sprinkle cinnamon on top. Bake at 350°F for about 30 minutes or until a toothpick inserted comes out with only a few crumbs attached.

# Honey Wheat Bread

*"One to eat, one to freeze, and one to give away," as my mother used to say. My mother started baking this bread in 1940 when she married my father. It is still a family favorite, with its tender crumb sweetened with honey.*

**2 tablespoons (18.6g) yeast, dissolved in 2 cups (473.18g) warm water**
**4–5 cups (480–600g) white bread flour, divided**
**4 teaspoons (22.76g) sea salt**
**1 tablespoon (12.38g) white sugar**
**½ cup (109g) oil**
**½ cup (170g) honey**
**½ cup (118.29g) warm water**
**2 cups (240g) whole-wheat flour**
**Melted butter, for pans and tops of bread**

1. Dissolve yeast in 2 cups warm water. Let rest until bubbly, about 5 minutes. Meanwhile, in the bowl of a stand mixer with paddle attachment, add 2 cups (240g) white bread flour, salt, and sugar. Pour the yeast mixture into this flour mixture and beat on low speed until smooth. Remove the paddle attachment, cover the bowl with a cloth, and let rise for about 45 minutes.

2. Remove the cloth and place back in the stand mixer, using the dough hook attachment. Add the oil, honey, and ½ cup (118.29g) of warm water. Turn the mixer on lowest speed and add the whole-wheat flour and 2 cups (240g) of bread flour. Dough should start coming together around the dough hook. Add up to 1 more cup of flour, if necessary, until dough no longer sticks to the bottom of the bowl. Remove the dough hook and scrape the sides of the bowl. Cover and let rise 30 minutes, and then punch down. Repeat twice.

3. At the final punch down, turn dough onto a floured surface. Divide it into 3 equal portions for small loaves, or 2 portions for large loaves. Knead each portion a few times, shape into a loaf, and press into a greased bread pan. Pierce with a fork. Cover and let rise until double in size.

4. Bake at 350°F for 30 minutes. When done, turn bread out of pans immediately onto cooling racks. Brush the tops with melted butter. When cool, place in an airtight bag. Will keep for 5 days. Makes 3 small loaves or 2 large loaves.

# Hungarian Walnut Strudel

*Treasured Amish and Mennonite Recipes*

*This traditional strudel recipe from the old country has been passed down through many generations of Amish and Mennonite women, likely coming from our European ancestors. It is made with a sweetened dough which contains a Walnut Filling tucked inside. My father loved to dunk these in hot chocolate.*

BREAD

**Dough**

½ cup (122g) lukewarm milk
1 package yeast (2¼ teaspoons, 7g)
1 tablespoon (12.38g) white sugar
1½ cups (180g) all-purpose flour (may need additional flour, up to ½ cup [60 g])
½ cup (113g) butter
3 large egg yolks (save whites for filling)
Juice from ½ lemon
2 tablespoons (24g) sour cream

**Walnut Filling**

8 ounces (234g) walnuts, ground
3 large egg whites
¾ cup (148.5g) white sugar
2 tablespoons (28g) fine dry breadcrumbs
1 pinch salt

1. For the dough, in a glass measuring cup, dissolve the sugar in lukewarm milk and sprinkle with the yeast. Let this rest for 10 minutes to allow the yeast to bloom. Meanwhile, in a medium mixing bowl, mix the flour and butter together with your hands until it resembles crumbs. Make a well in the flour mixture and add egg yolks, lemon juice, sour cream, and the yeast mixture. Mix by hand, adding more flour as needed to make a dough that doesn't stick to the fingers. Knead on a lightly floured board, rolling and folding until shiny.

2. For the **Walnut Filling**, beat the egg whites with the salt until they start to become stiff, then add the sugar gradually while beating. Fold in the ground walnuts and breadcrumbs.

**Assembly:** Cut the dough in half, then roll out one-half in a rectangle to ½-inch thickness and spread with one-half of the walnut filling. Roll up like a jelly roll and place edge down on a pan that has been buttered or lined with parchment paper. Repeat with the other half of the dough. Let rise for 1 hour. Brush with beaten egg yolk. Bake at 375°F for 30 minutes. Turn the oven off and let stand 15 minutes longer. Cool, then dust with confectioners' sugar and slice to serve.

BREAD

# Whole-Wheat Bread

*Amish Community Cookbook*

*A hearty wheat bread sweetened with honey that's perfect for slicing.*

**2 packages (4½ teaspoons, 14g) yeast**
**2¼ cups (532.32g) warm water, divided**
**⅓ cup (113.33g) honey**
**¼ cup (56.5g) butter or shortening**
**1 tablespoon (17.06g) salt**
**3 cups (360g) whole-wheat flour**
**3–4 cups (360–480g) white flour**

Dissolve yeast in ½ cup warm water and let it set for 5 minutes. Meanwhile, in the bowl of a stand mixer with the dough attachment, add the honey, shortening, salt, 1¾ cups warm water, the yeast mixture, and the whole-wheat flour. Beat until smooth. Mix in enough white flour to make a dough that's easy to handle and will pull away from the sides of the mixer bowl. Mix dough on low-to-medium speed for about 10 minutes. Remove dough and place in a buttered bowl. Cover and let rise in warm place until double, about 1 hour. Punch down and divide dough in half. Form 2 loaves and place in buttered baking pans. Let rise until double, about 1 hour. Bake at 350°F for 40 minutes or until loaves are golden and sound hollow when tapped on the bottom.

# Pumpkin Bread

*Filled with warm spices, this bread improves in taste by the second day if you can wait that long to eat it! It's delicious served plain or covered with Maple Frosting when cool. This recipe is dairy-free without the frosting.*

**3½ cups (420g) all-purpose flour**
**¾ teaspoon (3.75g) baking soda**
**1 teaspoon (5g) baking powder**
**1½ teaspoons (8.53g) sea salt**
**3 teaspoons (8.4g) ground cinnamon**
**1 teaspoon (2.1g) ground cloves**
**3 teaspoons (8.4g) ground ginger**
**¼ teaspoon (0.58g) ground black pepper**
**4 large eggs, beaten**
**1⅔ cups (333.3g) white sugar**
**1 cup (213g) brown sugar**
**2 cups (490g) pumpkin puree**
**⅔ cup (157.73g) water**
**½ cup (108.6g) oil**

***Maple Frosting: Page 188***

1. Sift together the flour, baking soda, baking powder, salt, and spices in a medium-sized bowl. In the bowl of a stand mixer, beat the eggs, then add the sugar, pumpkin, water, and oil and beat until blended. Slowly add the dry ingredients to the mixer bowl and mix until the flour is incorporated. Pour the batter into 2 buttered and floured 9 x 5-inch loaf pans. Bake at 350°F for approximately 40 minutes, or until a toothpick inserted in the center comes out with only a few crumbs attached.

2. For the **Maple Frosting**, see page 188. When Pumpkin Bread has completely cooled, smooth the frosting over the top of the loaves.

*This frosting will set up after it's whipped, so don't make it too far ahead of time.*

# Lemon Loaf with Rosemary Sugared Cranberries

*A tart citrus sweet bread I love to make around Thanksgiving when fresh cranberries are available. The yogurt in the batter keeps the bread wonderfully moist, and the sugared cranberries on top make the bread a beautiful presentation to give as a gift.*

***Rosemary Sugared Cranberries: Page 186***

**Lemon Loaf**

1 cup (200g) white sugar
1 tablespoon (6g) lemon zest
⅓ cup (72.4g) olive oil
2 large eggs, well beaten
½ cup (112g) whole milk, full-fat yogurt
¼ cup (85g) lemon juice
2 cups (240g) all-purpose flour
1 teaspoon (5g) baking powder
½ teaspoon (2.84g) salt
1 cup (99g) coarsely chopped fresh cranberries

**Lemon Glaze**

3 tablespoons (45g) freshly squeezed lemon juice
1½ cups (195g) confectioners' sugar, sifted

BREAD

1. Prepare the **Rosemary Sugared Cranberries**; see page 186.

2. For the **Lemon Loaf**: In the bowl of a stand mixer, combine the sugar and lemon zest, massaging them together with your hands to release the oils and aroma in the lemon zest. Add the oil, eggs, and yogurt and beat until blended. Whisk together the flour, baking powder, and salt and add to the mixer, along with the lemon juice. Lastly, add the chopped cranberries and beat just until blended, scraping the bowl. Pour into a 9 x 5-inch loaf pan that has been buttered and floured or lined with parchment paper. Bake at 350°F for about 45 minutes or until a toothpick inserted comes out clean or with only a few crumbs attached. Cool in the pan for 10 minutes, then remove to a cooling rack and cover with glaze.

3. For the **Lemon Glaze**: Whisk ingredients together until combined. Add more juice or more sugar to reach desired consistency. Decorate the loaf with sugared cranberries while the glaze is still sticky.

*I almost always bake 2 loaves of this bread because it disappears so quickly.*

# Crushed Wheat Bread

*Naomi Rabatin, Millersburg, Ohio (recipe adapted from His Saving Grains and Our Father's Foods)*

*This bread uses a flour called whole cell crushed wheat, which is milled in a unique patented process where the grains are crushed without destroying the cells. This is compatible for people with gluten sensitivities, as it is 100% natural with no synthetic food products. The flour can be sourced from various bulk food stores in Holmes County, Ohio, or may be purchased online.*

**2½ tablespoons (17.5g) ground flax**
**¼ cup (59.15g) water**
**4½ cups (1064.65g) lukewarm water**
**½ cup (108.59g) olive oil or coconut oil**
**⅔ cup (226.67g) honey**
**3 tablespoons (27g) instant yeast**
**1 tablespoon (22.5g) sunflower lecithin**
**2 tablespoons (34.14g) sea salt or Himalayan salt**
**6 cups (936g) crushed wheat #1 plus 5 cups (780g) crushed wheat #1, divided**
**¾ teaspoon (1.88g) xanthan gum**

1. Soak the ground flax in ¼ cup water for 5 minutes.

2. Mix lukewarm water, olive oil, and honey briefly on low with paddle attachment, then add instant yeast, sunflower lecithin, and Himalayan salt.

3. Mix briefly on low with paddle attachment, then add 6 cups of crushed wheat #1, the soaked flax, and xantham gum.

4. Mix 1 minute on low with paddle attachment, then add 5 cups of crushed wheat #1.

5. Switch to dough hook attachment and mix briefly on low, then add crushed wheat #1, ½ cup at a time until dough starts cleaning side of bowl. Continue adding small amounts of crushed wheat #1 until your dough is still very soft, but does not stick to hands. Mix for 10 minutes on low, then move dough to a greased mixing bowl and cover with cloth. Let rise for about 40 minutes.

6. Invert dough onto counter and divide into 6 loaves. Using a rolling pin, roll out dough about ¾-inch thick into a rectangle shape. Roll up and tuck inside and place in greased bread pans. Prick with fork. Let set in a warm place until dough has risen approximately 1½ inches above pans.

7. Bake at 325°F for approximately 30 minutes. Remove from pans and set on cooling racks. Brush with melted butter while still hot. Cool completely before bagging. Yields 6 loaves

# Buttered Biscuits

*These biscuits benefit from the fat in the butter and the whole milk, and the flaky layers are a result of folding the dough multiple times. Practice makes perfect when making biscuits, as well as a gentle touch and not over mixing the dough.*

**2 cups (240g) all-purpose flour**
**1 tablespoon (12g) baking powder**
**¾ teaspoon (4.26g) sea salt**
**2 tablespoons (24.75g) white sugar**
**½ cup (113g), plus 2 tablespoons (28.25g) unsalted butter, cold**
**1 large egg, fork beaten**
**⅔ cup (162.67g) whole milk**
**2 tablespoons (28.25g) melted butter for brushing the tops**

In a medium bowl, whisk dry ingredients together. Cut butter into cubes and work into the flour mixture with your fingers or a pastry cutter until only small chunks remain. Pour in milk and fork-beaten egg and gently stir until the dough comes together. Turn onto a floured surface and with your hands or a rolling pin, pat the dough gently into a 1-inch-think rectangle. Fold in half. Pat into a rectangle again and fold in half again. Repeat the folding and patting process for a total of 5 times. Then, using a biscuit cutter, cut out circles about ¾–1 inch thick and place on a baking sheet covered with parchment paper. Brush tops liberally with melted butter. Bake at 415°F for about 10 minutes until puffed and golden. Makes about 8–10 medium-sized biscuits.

# Corn Pone

*Grandma Linda Gingerich, Millersburg, Ohio*

*Corn pone was a staple in my husband's family growing up. They ate it in bowls with milk for breakfast or dinner. These days, it is more common to eat it slathered with butter and honey, like cornbread.*

**3 cups (360g) all-purpose flour**
**¾ cup (150g) white sugar**
**2 cups (312g) cornmeal**
**1½ teaspoons (9g) baking soda**
**¾ cup (154.2g) oil**
**2 large eggs, fork-beaten**
**2 cups (488g) milk**

Whisk dry ingredients in a bowl. In a separate bowl, whisk the eggs, oil, and milk. Pour this into the flour mixture and whisk until combined. Pour into a buttered 9 x 12-inch baking dish and bake at 350°F for about 25-30 minutes until toothpick inserted in center comes out with only crumbs attached.

# Banana Bread

*A favorite after-school snack, this Banana Bread is a great way to use leftover bananas when they have passed their prime for eating. Sprinkling sugar on top of the dough before you slide it in the oven creates a crackly crust that adds to the flavor and texture.*

**2 cups (426g) brown sugar**
**½ cup (113g) unsalted butter, room temperature**
**2 large eggs, room temperature**
**3 cups (360g) all-purpose flour**
**1½ teaspoons (9g) baking soda**
**¾ teaspoon (4.27g) sea salt**
**½ cup (112g) buttermilk**
**1 teaspoon (4.34g) pure vanilla extract**
**4 large bananas, mashed**
**White sugar, for sprinkling**

In the bowl of a stand mixer, beat the sugar and butter for about 4 minutes. Then, add the eggs, one at a time, and beat until incorporated. In a separate bowl, whisk together the flour, baking soda, and salt, then add slowly along with the buttermilk and vanilla. Last, fold in the bananas and stir until blended. Pour into a 9 x 5-inch loaf pan that has been buttered and floured or lined with parchment paper. Sprinkle white sugar over the dough, if desired. Bake at 325°F for about 45–55 minutes, until a toothpick inserted in center comes out with only a few crumbs attached.

# Singing

*Singing plays a significant role in the Amish lifestyle and culture, and it is an essential part of their worship in the church. Hymns and spiritual songs are sung a cappella (without music), to show their simplicity and humility to Jesus. The Amish hymnals, known as* Gesangbuchs, *have songs that reflect Amish religious beliefs. Singing hymns allows them to join their voices in praise and worship, fostering a sense of unity and spiritual connection. They do so through four-part harmony, shape-note singing, slow tempos, and reverence, participation, and community.*

I remember sitting on the couch with my mother at the age of five as she taught me the musical notes, "DO, RE, MI, FA, SOL, LA, TI, DO." We sang them together, up and down, repeatedly. Singing was important to her, and she taught each of her five children to appreciate singing in four-part harmony.

We often sang together in our home, especially before mealtimes when we had guests. We would gather around the table and sing in four-part harmony the hymn by C. B. Widmeyer, "Come and Dine," and then my father would pray for the meal.

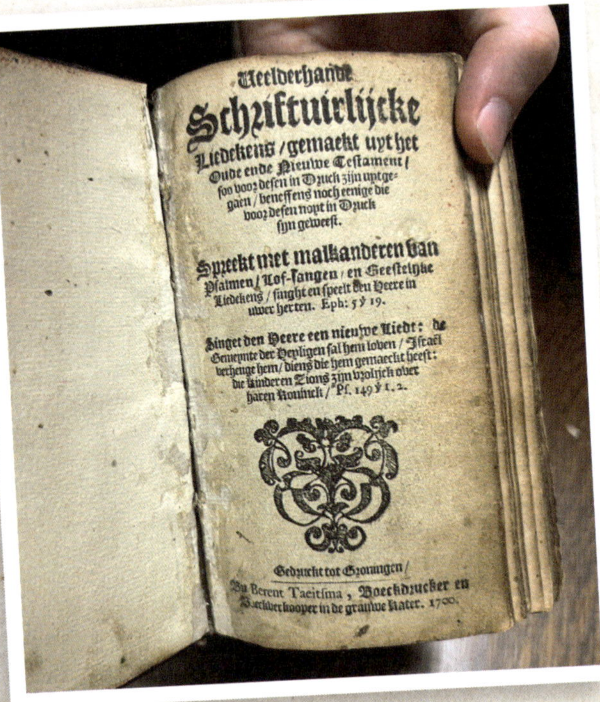


This Dutch Hymnal from the 1700s was brought from Holland to America by one of my ancestors and passed down to my father. It now resides in the museum at the Amish and Mennonite Information Center in Berlin, Ohio.

*Jesus has a table spread, where the saints of God are fed,*
*He invites his chosen people, "Come and dine."*
*With his manna he doth feed and supplies our every need*
*O 'tis sweet to sup with Jesus all the time.*
*"Come and dine," the Master calleth, "Come and dine."*
*You may feast at Jesus' table all the time*
*He who fed the multitude, turned the water into wine,*
*To the hungry calleth now, "Come and dine."*

During Sunday services, I sat beside my mother at a young age, blending in my alto voice with hers as we sang hymns out of the church hymnal. And since there was segregated seating—the men on one side of the church and the women on the other side—there were some Sundays when I sat beside my father. He sang in a beautiful bass tone while my older brothers joined with their tenor voices. Singing was my favorite part of church services, and I learned every verse of every song through many years of congregational singing.

## Christmas Caroling

*The Amish celebrate Christmas with honor, simplicity, and tradition, keeping their focus on the birth of Jesus. And because it is a festive occasion, the Amish celebrate by caroling. They enjoy singing for older people in their community who might be infirm or widowed to bring joy into their lives. They do not sing secular Christmas carols like "Rudolph the Red-Nosed Reindeer" or "Frosty the Snowman." Rather, they sing songs like "Away in a Manger" and "The First Noel."*

Every December I looked forward to Christmas caroling, which was hosted by our church. The ladies would all get together during the day to pack generous boxes of food which we would distribute during caroling to the widows of our congregation, needy families, and to our ministers. The boxes were filled with a Christmas ham, canned goods, a variety of freshly baked Christmas cookies and confections, homemade bread, oranges, and apples.

In the evening of that same day, we piled in vans with boxes loaded in the back and drove across the country roads to our various destinations. Often it was cold and snowy, as Ohio Decembers generally are, and we would stand outside homes in a winter wonderland singing carols such as "Silent Night," "Joy to the World," "O Come, All Ye Faithful," and others. We always wrapped up by singing "We Wish You a Merry Christmas," and then someone would ring the doorbell and deliver the box of food into welcoming hands. Afterwards, we all met up at the church for cookies and hot chocolate. Another treat for me when I came home was to dig through our own Christmas box, since my father was the bishop and we always received one.

# CHAPTER 6

In our home growing up, breakfast was always a time when our family sat down together around the table. After the cows were milked, Father would come in, wash his hands, and begin the ritual of making a delicious, stick-to-the-ribs meal. While he may have skimped on dinner sometimes by eating a bowl of corn flakes, when it came to breakfast, he wanted a warm and hearty meal to start the day. And he knew how to cook it.

While Mother cooked most meals in our home, Father was often the one at the stove in the morning. I remember waking up to the sounds of him frying eggs or making pancakes. Often there was bacon or sausage and hash browns, and sometimes we would have fried mush to eat with honey or tomato gravy. Regardless of the variety, there was always a small kettle of Cream of Wheat® or rolled oats cooking on the back burner, which we ate with milk and a generous helping of brown sugar.

*Mary, a tiny Amish widow with rosy cheeks and a snowy cap, operated a bakery in her farmhouse kitchen.*

We'd gather around the table with steaming plates of food, then bow our heads while Father prayed a blessing over the meal and our day. After breakfast was over, we had a tradition of quoting a chapter in Psalms which we would memorize over the course of a week, through repetition, and then we cleared the table, washed the dishes, and went on with our day.

These days, I talk with many people who tell me they don't eat breakfast. Or if they do, it may be just a piece of toast or a sweet pastry from a local bakery. While I understand the appeal of a cinnamon roll for breakfast, it will never replace the full breakfasts that filled my belly as a child.

Cinnamon rolls definitely had a place in my life, though, and my father and I had a weekly tradition of bouncing across gravel roads to our neighbor's house for this treat. Mary, a tiny Amish widow with rosy cheeks and a snowy cap, operated a bakery in her farmhouse kitchen. Her cinnamon rolls were the highlight of my week. We would lean against her counter eating rolls pulled straight from the wood-fired oven, frosting dripping on chin and fingers as we conversed in our Pennsylvania Dutch dialect. Later, we drove back to our own farmhouse, a pan of rolls between us.

When I started a family of my own, those heritage cinnamon rolls remained a part of our tradition as I baked them from scratch in my kitchen. And years later when my daughter and I started a bakery, they became our signature product (How to Make Sour Cream Cinnamon Rolls, page 152). Now, people travel from all over to make them a part of their weekly tradition as well.

So, whether you start your day with bacon and eggs, a bowl of oatmeal, or even a piece of toast and the occasional cinnamon roll, I hope you enjoy this collection of breakfast recipes. And while I realize it's harder these days for families to start their day around the table together, perhaps you will find time on weekends to create a tradition of family breakfast.

## • RECIPES •

# Breakfast

BREAKFAST

# How to Make Sour Cream Cinnamon Rolls

*Everyone loves a good cinnamon roll, and this step-by-step process will help you make them in your home kitchen. The dough is enriched with mashed potatoes and sour cream, which keeps them fluffy. These are sized to be fat and chunky, but if you prefer a smaller roll, divide the dough in half to make 24 rolls instead of 12. While this is not the recipe we use at our bakery, it is still a delicious cinnamon roll.*

## Ingredients

2 packages (4½ teaspoons, 12g) yeast
¾ cup (176.49g) warm water
½ cup (113g) unsalted butter
1 cup (249g) sour cream, room temperature
1 teaspoon (5.69g) sea salt
1 cup (213g) mashed potatoes
½ cup (101g) white sugar
1 large egg
5½ cups (600g) all-purpose flour

### Inside the Rolls

4 tablespoons (56.52g) melted butter (save some for brushing pan)
½ cup (82.5g) brown sugar
Cinnamon, to taste

**1. Gather all your ingredients together.** Activate the yeast in warm water and set it in a cozy spot for about 5 minutes until the top starts to look bubbly. Meanwhile, in a medium saucepan, melt the butter over low heat. Turn off the heat and add the sour cream, salt, mashed potatoes, and sugar. Stir together, then pour into the bowl of a stand mixer.

**2.** With the dough hook attachment and on low speed, add the egg, 2 cups of flour, and the yeast mixture. Mix until the dough looks smooth, then slowly add the remaining flour, up to 3½ cups, until the dough pulls away from the sides of the bowl and the dough is soft to the touch but does not stick to your hands. Turn the dough out onto a floured counter and knead for 30 seconds. Place the dough into a buttered bowl and cover with a cloth. Let it rise until doubled in size, approximately 1 hour, depending on the warmth of your kitchen.

**3.** After the dough has doubled in size, make a fist with your hand and gently punch down the dough to deflate the air.

**4.** Roll the dough into a rectangle, brush with melted butter, and sprinkle with brown sugar and cinnamon.

**5.** Roll up the dough tightly like a jelly roll.

**6.** Slice the roll into 12 pieces.

**7.** Butter two 9-inch (23cm) baking pans or one 9 x 13-inch pan and place the rolls in the pan.

**8.** Let the rolls rise for about 30–40 minutes (depending on the warmth of your kitchen).

**9.** Bake the rolls at 345°F for about 20–25 minutes until lightly browned. Cover with aluminum foil if they are getting too brown during the baking process. Cool slightly and frost with your favorite frosting. (I recommend the Maple Frosting on page 188).

With my father, Andrew D. Stutzman, in 1964.

# Sour Cream Coffee Cake

*Ruth Mast, Hopewell, Ohio*

*This recipe from my sister is one of the best coffee cakes I've tasted. The addition of sour cream keeps the texture of the cake soft and moist.*

**1 cup (226g) butter, softened**
**1 cup (200g) white sugar**
**3 large eggs, room temperature**
**1 cup (250g) sour cream, room temperature**
**1½ teaspoon (7.5g) pure vanilla extract**
**3 cups (360g) all-purpose flour**
**½ teaspoon (3g) baking soda**
**3 teaspoons (12g) baking powder**

**Cinnamon Sugar**
**2 teaspoons (14g) ground cinnamon**
**1 cup (150g) finely chopped nuts**
**½ cup (100g) white sugar**

1. For the **Cinnamon Sugar**, mix ingredients together in a bowl. Set aside.

2. Cream the butter and the sugar, then add the eggs, one at a time. Beat until combined, then add the sour cream and vanilla. Mix until combined and then scrape the bowl. In a medium bowl, whisk together the flour, baking soda, and baking powder and add to the mixture. Beat just until streaks of flour have disappeared. Pour this batter into two 8-inch round buttered cake pans (or one 10-inch square pan), alternating with the Cinnamon Sugar mixture. Bake at 350°F for about 30 minutes if divided into 2 pans, or for about 55 minutes if baked in one pan. When a toothpick inserted in the center comes out with a few crumbs attached, it's ready.

# Cinnamon Sugar Coffee Cake

*Laura Mast, Millersburg, Ohio*

*The appeal of this cinnamon-swirled coffee cake is the creamy glaze poured over the top when it has cooled slightly.*

2 cups (240g) all-purpose flour
½ teaspoon (2.84g) sea salt
½ teaspoon (4g) baking powder
½ teaspoon (3g) baking soda
1¼ cups (250g) white sugar
1 cup (217.18g) oil
2 large eggs
1 teaspoon (5g) pure vanilla extract
1 cup (224g) whole fat buttermilk

**Cinnamon Brown Sugar**
4 tablespoons (53.25g) brown sugar
1 tablespoon (7g) ground cinnamon

**Glaze**
2 cups (230g) confectioners' sugar
1 teaspoon (5g) pure vanilla extract

1. Whisk the flour, salt, baking powder, and baking soda in a bowl and set aside. In the bowl of a stand mixer, mix the sugar and the oil. Add the eggs and mix until blended, then add the buttermilk alternately with the flour mixture and beat just until blended, scraping bowl a few times in the process.

2. Pour batter alternately with Cinnamon Sugar into a 9 x 12-inch buttered cake pan. Bake for approximately 20 minutes at 350°F until a toothpick inserted comes out with only crumbs attached. Cool for 5 minutes, then pour Glaze over cake while it is still warm.

3. For the **Glaze**, mix the 2 ingredients in a bowl and then add enough milk by the tablespoon to make a pourable glaze.

# Blueberry Streusel Coffee Cake

*Using yogurt to add moisture, this coffee cake is loaded with blueberries and covered with a streusel topping.*

1 cup (226g) butter, room temperature
1 cup (200g) white sugar
3 large eggs, room temperature
1 cup (224g) whole milk yogurt, room temperature
1½ teaspoons (7.5g) pure vanilla extract
3 cups (360g) all-purpose flour
½ teaspoon (3g) baking soda
3 teaspoons (12g) baking powder
½ teaspoon (2.84g) sea salt
1½ cups (225g) fresh blueberries

**Streusel Topping**

¾ cup (90g) all-purpose flour
½ cup (100g) white sugar
3 tablespoons (42.38g) butter, melted
1 teaspoon (7g) ground cinnamon

BREAKFAST

1. In the bowl of a stand mixer, cream together the butter and sugar for about 3 minutes. Then, add the eggs, yogurt, and vanilla. Whisk together the dry ingredients and add them slowly. Mix just until incorporated. With a spoon or spatula gently stir in the blueberries.

2. Pour batter into a 9 x 13-inch buttered cake pan or into two 8-inch round buttered pie pans. Cover with the Streusel Topping and bake at 350°F for about 30 minutes, or until a toothpick inserted comes out with just a few crumbs attached. May require additional bake time if baked in one pan.

3. For the **Streusel Topping**, stir ingredients together with a fork and then mix with your hands until it turns into fine crumbs.

# Raspberry Scones

*There is a trick to making good scones, and the dough needs to be handled like biscuits and pie dough. A delicate touch as you bring the ingredients together goes a long way towards a tender scone. You may swap out the raspberries in these scones for other fresh berries, such as strawberries, blackberries, or blueberries.*

- 3 cups (360g) all-purpose flour
- ⅓ cup (66g) white sugar
- 2 teaspoons (8g) baking powder
- ½ teaspoon (3g) baking soda
- 1 teaspoon (5.68g) sea salt
- ½ cup (113g) unsalted butter, cold
- 1 large egg
- 1 cup (224g) buttermilk or heavy cream
- 1 teaspoon (5g) pure vanilla extract
- 1 cup (120g) fresh raspberries, pulled apart into halves

**Lemon Glaze**

- 1 cup (113.5g) confectioners' sugar
- The freshly squeezed juice of 1 lemon

1. In a medium-sized bowl, sift together the flour, sugar, baking powder, baking soda, and salt. Cut the cold butter into 1-inch cubes and then, with your fingers or a pastry cutter, work it into the flour mixture until the dough resembles coarse crumbs with some small butter chunks visible. Make a well in the center of the dough. In a small bowl, stir together the buttermilk or cream, the egg, and vanilla until blended, then pour into the well. With a large wooden spoon or a spatula, gently fold the milk mixture into the dough. When it is almost incorporated, add the raspberries and finish with the last few folds or stirs. Turn the dough out onto the counter and gently pat into an 8-inch circle. Cut into 8 pie-shaped pieces and place on a parchment-lined baking sheet. Chill in the refrigerator for about 30 minutes prior to baking.

2. For the **Lemon Glaze**, whisk together ingredients and set aside to drizzle over cooled scones.

3. When scones have chilled, brush their tops with buttermilk or cream and sprinkle with coarse sugar. Bake at 400°F for 10 minutes, then rotate the tray, reduce heat to 325°F, and bake for an additional 7–8 minutes. Allow scones to cool slightly before drizzling with Lemon Glaze.

# Buttermilk Waffles

*Ruth Rabatin, Millersburg, Ohio*

*These fluffy waffles are a perfect weekend breakfast, whether served with butter and maple syrup, or whipped cream and fresh fruit. The fluffiness comes from whipping the eggs whites and folding them into the batter last. To keep waffles from getting limp, place them in single layer on a cooling rack to allow steam to escape instead of placing them all on a stack as you make them.*

**2 cups (240g) wheat flour or all-purpose flour**
**2 teaspoons (8g) baking powder**
**1 teaspoon (6g) baking soda**
**1 teaspoon (5.68g) sea salt**
**2 tablespoons (26.63g) brown sugar**
**3 large eggs (separated)**
**2 cups (448g) buttermilk**
**¼ cup (48g) oil**

In a medium bowl, whisk together the dry ingredients. In a separate bowl, beat the egg whites to a creamy texture and set aside. To the bowl of dry ingredients, add the egg yolks, buttermilk, and oil, stirring to combine. Lastly, fold in the beaten egg whites. Use ½-¾ cup of batter at a time in a waffle maker. They will get nice and fluffy! Makes 8-10 waffles.

# Maple Granola

*Sweetened with maple syrup and no additional sugars, this granola is perfect to eat for breakfast, lunch, or a bedtime snack. It's delicious with milk, or as a topping for yogurt or cottage cheese.*

**4 cups (360g) organic old-fashioned oats**
**1½ cups (192g) pecans, chopped coarsely**
**½ cup (70g) sunflower seeds**
**1 teaspoon (4.93g) sea salt**
**1 teaspoon (2.6g) ground cinnamon**
**1 teaspoon (2.6g) ginger**
**½ teaspoon (1.3g) cardamom**
**½ cup (80g) dried blueberries**
**½ cup (120g) maple syrup**
**½ cup (108.59g) olive oil**
**1 teaspoon (4.2g) maple extract**

In a medium-sized bowl, stir together the oats, pecans, sunflower seeds, salt, and spices. Then, in a small saucepan, heat the maple syrup and olive oil, just to boiling. Remove from heat and stir in the maple extract. Pour over the oat mixture and stir thoroughly to coat the granola evenly. Pour onto a parchment-lined baking sheet (16 x 12 inches) and bake at 350°F for 25 minutes, stirring once during the baking process. Remove from the oven and stir in the dried blueberries. Let it rest on the pan until it has thoroughly cooled, then scoop into an airtight container.

BREAKFAST

# Blueberry Lemon Muffins

*These Blueberry Lemon Muffins are not overly sweet and are delicious on their own or cut in half and spread with butter. They are my grandsons' favorites.*

- 2 large eggs, at room temperature
- ⅔ cup (132g) white sugar
- 2 cups (240g) all-purpose flour
- 1 tablespoon (12g) baking powder
- 1 teaspoon (5.69g) sea salt
- 2 tablespoons (12g) lemon zest
- 2 tablespoons (30g) lemon juice
- ½ cup (113g) unsalted butter, melted
- 1 cup (250g) full-fat sour cream, at room temperature
- 2 cups (300g) fresh or frozen blueberries

**Streusel Topping**

- 3 tablespoons (42.38g) unsalted butter, melted
- ¾ cup (90g) all-purpose flour
- ¼ cup (49.5g) white sugar
- ⅓ cup (71g) brown sugar
- 1 pinch of salt

1. In the bowl of a stand mixer, whisk the eggs. Meanwhile, in a separate bowl, mix the white sugar with the lemon zest. Massage the zest into the sugar. Then, to this bowl, add the flour, baking powder, and salt and whisk all together. Set aside. In the mixer bowl with the beaten eggs, add the sour cream, lemon juice, and melted butter, then slowly add the dry ingredients from your bowl and stir just until blended. Fold in the fresh blueberries. Fill lined cupcake pans approximately ¾ full of batter, then top with the Streusel Mixture.

2. For the **Streusel Mixture**, toss ingredients with a fork to create crumbs.

3. Bake at 385°F for 10 minutes. Rotate pans, reduce heat to 375°F and bake for an additional 8-10 minutes. If using larger muffin pans, adjust bake time accordingly. Serve with scoops of salted butter.

# Cream-Filled Coffee Cake

*Michelle Gingerich, Sugarcreek, Ohio*

*This is an old-fashioned sweet dough recipe from our Amish community in Holmes County, Ohio. After baking, the coffee cakes are cut in half and spread with a layer of cream filling.*

BREAKFAST

- 2¼ teaspoons (7g) dry yeast
- ½ cup (118.29g) warm water
- 1 cup (244g) milk
- 1 stick (113g) butter
- ½ cup (99g) white sugar
- 1 teaspoon (5.69g) sea salt
- 2 large eggs, beaten
- 3½ cups (420g) all-purpose flour

**Crumb Topping**

- ⅓ cup (71g) brown sugar
- ⅓ cup (40g) all-purpose flour
- 2 tablespoons (28.25g) butter
- 1 teaspoon (7g) ground cinnamon
- ½ cup (75g) finely chopped nuts

**Cream Filling**

- 5 tablespoons (37.5g) all-purpose flour
- 1 cup (244g) whole milk
- 1 cup (226g) butter, softened to room temperature
- 3 cups (345g) confectioners' sugar, sifted

1. Heat the milk and the butter until it's steaming, then cool until lukewarm. While milk is cooling, dissolve yeast in warm water and let it set for 5 minutes. When the milk and butter mixture is lukewarm, put it in the bowl of a stand mixer and add the yeast mixture, sugar, salt, beaten eggs, flour, and vanilla. Mix until blended. Turn out the dough onto the counter to knead a few times, then place in a buttered bowl. Cover the bowl with a cloth and let it rise until it has doubled in size. Punch down the dough, then turn it onto the counter again and divide it into 3 portions. Place each dough portion in an 8-inch round cake pan. Sprinkle with Crumb Topping and let rise again for about 20–30 minutes. Bake at 350°F for about 20–25 minutes until lightly browned.

2. For the **Cream Filling**, whisk together the flour and the milk. Pour into a saucepan and cook until thick, whisking constantly. Remove from heat and cool. Meanwhile, beat the butter until creamy (about 5 minutes) and slowly add the confectioners' sugar. Then, add the cooked filling and beat until well blended.

**Assembly:** Cut each coffee cake circle in half. Spread Cream Filling on bottom half and cover with top half.

# Baked French Toast

*This delicious Baked French Toast rests in the refrigerator overnight and is ready for the oven in the morning. It is drizzled with a caramelized pecan topping and bakes up fluffy like a soufflé.*

**1 fat loaf French or brioche bread, cut into thick slices**
**8 large eggs**
**2 cups (488g) whole milk**
**2 cups (488g) half-and-half**
**2 teaspoons (8.4g) pure vanilla extract**
**½ teaspoon (1.3g) cinnamon**
**½ teaspoon (1.3g) nutmeg**

### Pecan Topping

**½ cup (113g) butter, melted**
**1 cup (213g) brown sugar**
**1 cup pecans, chopped**

Butter a 9 x 13-inch baking pan and arrange bread slices in the pan. In the bowl of a stand mixer, beat the eggs, milk, half-and-half, vanilla, and spices. Pour the mixture over the bread slices. Cover and refrigerate overnight. The next morning, make the topping by combining the butter, sugar, and pecans. Drizzle over the pan of French toast. Bake at 350°F for about 35–40 minutes, until puffed and golden. Serve with maple syrup. Serves 8.

# Buttermilk Pancakes

*Amish Community Cookbook*

*A staple for weekend breakfasts, the addition of buttermilk adds a tang to these delicious pancakes, and the whipped egg whites keep them fluffy.*

**2 cups (240g) all-purpose flour**
**1 teaspoon (5g) baking powder**
**½ teaspoon (2.84g) salt**
**1 teaspoon (6g) baking soda**
**2 teaspoons (8.25g) white sugar**
**2 cups (448g) buttermilk**
**2 large eggs, separated**
**3 tablespoons (42.38g) butter, melted**

In a medium bowl, whisk together the dry ingredients. Then, add the buttermilk, the egg yolks, and the melted butter, stirring until blended. Lastly, fold in the beaten egg whites. Scoop by ½ cup into a buttered skillet. Serve with maple syrup and garnish with fruit or confectioners' sugar, as desired.

# Potato Cinnamon Rolls

*Esther Miller, Mt. Hope, Ohio*

*The addition of mashed potatoes in this recipe keeps the rolls soft and fluffy. Additionally, you can divide the dough in half, saving a portion in the refrigerator to make the following day.*

**⅔ cup (138g) shortening**
**1 cup (230g) mashed potatoes**
**½ cup (118.29g) lukewarm water**
**2¼ teaspoons (7g) dry yeast**
**½ cup (99g) white sugar**
**6–8 cups (720–960g) of all-purpose flour**
**1 teaspoon (5.69g) sea salt**
**2 large eggs**
**1 cup (244g) milk, scalded**

***Maple Frosting: Page 188***

1. Put yeast in lukewarm water and let it set for about 5 minutes. Cream shortening, potatoes, and sugar. Add eggs and beat well. Add salt and milk and mix well. Add yeast water and stir in flour. Add enough flour so dough is soft but not sticky. Cover the dough and let it rise until double in size.

2. Divide the dough in half. Roll out into a rectangle, brush with melted butter, and sprinkle with brown sugar and cinnamon. Roll up tightly like a jelly roll. Cut each roll into 12 slices. Place cinnamon rolls on a buttered half-sheet pan. Repeat with the other half of the dough, or you may refrigerate the other half to use within 2 days.

3. Let rise for 20–30 minutes, then bake at 350°F for 20–25 minutes until lightly browned. Frost while still a little warm.

4. For the **Maple Frosting**, see page 188.

**Note:** If frosting becomes too thick, warm gently on stove or in microwave until it reaches spreadable consistency.

# Raised Donuts

*Esther Miller, Mt. Hope, Ohio*

*As a kid, I would stand beside my Amish Aunt Elizabeth as she fried these donuts over her wood-burning stove. The smell of wood smoke, kerosene lanterns, and sizzling fat mingled to provide a tantalizing aroma as I waited impatiently for them to cool. Homemade glazed donuts are simply the best, and this recipe is soft and airy and delicious.*

**4½ teaspoons (13.5g) yeast, dissolved in ⅓ cup (80g) warm water**
**½ cup (113g) lard or butter, melted and cooled**
**½ cup (100g) white sugar**
**1 teaspoon (6g) sea salt**
**½ cup (105g) mashed potatoes**
**3 large egg yolks**
**6½ cups (780g) flour, divided**
**2 cups (498g) milk, lukewarm**

### Glaze

**5 cups (625g) sifted confectioners' sugar**
**1 cup (236.59g) water**
**1 teaspoon (4.2g) pure vanilla extract**

1. Dissolve yeast in warm water and let it bloom for about 5–10 minutes. In the bowl of a stand mixer, with the paddle attachment, mix the butter, sugar, salt, mashed potatoes, egg yolks, and 2 cups (240g) of flour. Switch to the dough hook and add the yeast mixture, then gradually add the milk and the rest of the flour. (You may not need all the flour, so add a little at a time. Dough should be soft and just a little bit sticky.)

2. With the mixer on low speed, mix until the dough starts pulling away from the side of the bowl. Scrape the sides, then mix thoroughly (5–7 minutes). Scrape dough into a buttered bowl, cover and let rise in a cozy space until double in size, about 1 hour. Punch down the dough, then roll out to 1-inch thickness. Cut out and remove holes and place on a floured baking tray. Let rise again (approximately 30 minutes). Fry in 375°F (191°C) oil, 1 minute per side.

3. To make the **Glaze**, combine ingredients in a bowl and mix thoroughly.

4. While the donuts are warm, dip in Glaze (both sides) and rest on a raised tray on a rack. Glaze will dry in about 15-20 minutes.

# Baked Oatmeal

*Ruth Rabatin, Millersburg, Ohio*

*As an alternative to cooking oatmeal on the stovetop, this easy oven recipe serves up a healthy breakfast and is delicious when paired with yogurt or fruit.*

**1 cup (213g) brown sugar**
**3 cups (300g) oats**
**2 teaspoons (8g) baking powder**
**1 teaspoon (5.69g) salt**
**½ cup (113g) melted butter**
**2 large eggs, beaten**
**1 cup (244g) milk**

Whisk together dry ingredients, then add the butter, eggs, and milk. Stir well and pour into a greased 1½-quart casserole dish. Bake at 350°F for 30 minutes.

# Oatmeal Flapjacks

*Katelynn Rabatin, Millersburg, Ohio*

*A perfect choice for a Saturday morning family breakfast, these hearty flapjacks are delicious served with maple syrup and peanut butter. The batter can be stored up to 24 hours in the refrigerator.*

**½ cup (122g) milk**
**1 tablespoon (21.25g) honey**
**2 cups (448g) buttermilk**
**1½ cups (150g) oats**
**1 cup (120g) whole-wheat flour**
**½ teaspoon (2.84g) sea salt**
**1 teaspoon (5g) baking soda**
**2 large eggs, beaten**

In a medium bowl, mix the milk, honey, and buttermilk, then add the beaten eggs. Whisk together the oats, flour, salt, and baking soda and add to the liquid. Stir until blended. Drop by ¼ cup into a hot, buttered skillet. Yields 14–16 small flapjacks or 8 large flapjacks.

# Morning Glory Muffins

*Amish Community Cookbook*

*You can eat breakfast on the go, if you must, with one or two of these muffins packed with good things like carrots, nuts, apples, and raisins.*

2 cups (240g) all-purpose flour
1¼ cups (250g) white sugar
2 teaspoons (10g) baking soda
2 teaspoons (5.6g) cinnamon
½ teaspoon (2.95g) sea salt
3 large eggs, beaten
1 cup (216g) oil
2 teaspoons (8.6g) pure vanilla extract
2 cups (220g) grated carrots
½ cup (85g) raisins
½ cup (56.5g) shredded coconut
½ cup (150g) chopped nuts
1 apple, shredded

Combine flour, sugar, baking soda, cinnamon, and salt. Mix thoroughly. Beat together the eggs, oil, and vanilla. Blend into the flour mixture. Fold in the carrots, raisins, coconut, nuts, and shredded apple. Bake at 350°F for 18 minutes or until a toothpick comes out with only crumbs attached. Yields 22 small muffins

# Maple Baked Oatmeal with Roasted Fruit

*This warmly spiced oatmeal uses less sugar and is delicious when served with roasted blueberries, strawberries, or peaches.*

3 cups (300g) oats
½ cup (106.5g) brown sugar
½ teaspoon (1.4g) ground cinnamon
2 teaspoons (10g) baking powder
1 pinch salt
½ cup (156g) maple syrup
½ cup (108.59g) oil
1 cup (244g) whole milk
2 large eggs, beaten
1½ teaspoons (6.45g) pure vanilla extract

**Roasted Fruit**

2 cups fresh fruit (blueberries, strawberries, or sliced peaches)
¼ cup sugar

1. In a mixing bowl, stir together the oats, sugar, cinnamon, baking powder, and salt. Then, add the maple syrup, oil, milk, beaten eggs, and vanilla. Mix with a spoon until blended. Pour into a buttered baking pan, either an 8 x 8-inch square or a 9-inch round. Bake for 30 minutes at 350°F. Serve warm.

2. For the **Roasted Fruit**: Toss fruit in a bowl with the sugar, then roast on a pan in the oven until juicy, about 8–10 minutes at 400°F. Serve over the oatmeal with milk or yogurt.

*You can also stir 1 cup of fresh fruit into the batter and bake it with the oatmeal.*

# Breakfast Crêpes

*Adapted slightly from a recipe by Naomi Rabatin, Millersburg, Ohio*

*These crêpes are delicious when rolled up and baked with sauteed mushrooms, spinach, and cheese, or filled with scrambled eggs and topped with salsa. My favorite way of making them is to fill them with a cream cheese mixture and then top with Blueberry Compote (page 190) and whipped cream. Guests feel incredibly pampered with this dish! If you have never made crêpes, I will say that practice makes perfect. I have included some tips below.*

**1¾ cups (210g) all-purpose flour**
**½ teaspoon (2.84g) salt**
**2 cups (488g) whole milk**
**3 large eggs**
**5 tablespoons (70.62g) butter, melted**

**Cream Cheese Filling**

**12 ounces (340.19g) cream cheese, softened**
**½ cup (65g) powdered sugar**
**1 teaspoon (4.3g) pure vanilla extract**
**½ teaspoon (1.3g) ground cinnamon**

1. In a medium-sized bowl, whisk together the flour and salt. In another bowl, whisk the eggs and milk. Slowly whisk the egg/milk mixture into the flour mixture until smooth, then whisk in the melted butter. Pour mixture ½ cup at a time into the center of skillet, swirling the pan to spread out the batter. When the first side is starting to look dry, flip it over gently to heat the other side. Remove from the pan and lay on a cookie sheet lined with parchment paper. Continue until all the batter is used, stacking the crêpes with parchment or wax paper in between. When all the crêpes have been cooked, fill with your choice of stuffing and roll them up. Nestle them single layer in a baking pan and bake at 350°F for about 15 minutes.

2. For the **Cream Cheese Filling**: In the bowl of a stand mixer, whip the cream cheese and confectioners' sugar until fluffy. Scrape the bowl, then add the vanilla and cinnamon and beat again until combined. Spread Cream Cheese Filling inside each crêpe, and roll. When baked, plate them with a spoonful of Blueberry Compote (page 190) and whipped cream, or garnish with the fruit of your choice.

## Tips

1. Prepare your skillet (10 inches). A non-stick pan works great, although I like to use a well-seasoned cast iron. Turn the heat to medium low and allow the pan to get hot before you add the batter. Brush it lightly with olive oil or cooking spray. You may only need to do this one time, if your pan is well seasoned.

2. Pour a small amount of batter into the center of the skillet and then slowly tip the pan all around in a circular motion to spread the batter thinly around the skillet within an inch or two of the edges.

3. They are fragile to turn over but if you wait until the top begins to look dry before you flip it, things will go easier.

# Pumpkin Spice Muffins

*Treasured Amish and Mennonite Recipes*

*A handheld treat that is moist and delicious with warm spices and pumpkin puree. You can either drizzle them with a simple glaze or eat them plain. I omitted the raisins and nuts, but they can be added for extra texture.*

2 large eggs
½ cup (100g) sugar
¾ cup (187.5g) canned pumpkin
¼ cup (54g) oil
1½ cups (180g) flour
1 teaspoon (4.8g) baking powder
½ teaspoon (2.4g) baking soda
½ teaspoon (3g) salt
¼ teaspoon (0.65g) cinnamon
¼ teaspoon (0.65g) cloves
¼ teaspoon nutmeg
¾ cup (120g) raisins (optional)
½ cup (75g) chopped nuts (optional)

**Glaze**

1 cup (110g) confectioners' sugar
2 tablespoons (30g) milk

1. In a medium mixing bowl, stir together the eggs, sugar, pumpkin, and oil. Whisk together the dry ingredients and then stir into the wet mixture. Mix until blended. Spoon batter into muffin tins (fill cups ¾ full). Bake at 375°F for about 15 minutes. Yields 10–12 regular-size muffins

2. For the **Glaze**, stir ingredients together, and drizzle over cupcakes.

# Granola and Yogurt Cups

*I was first introduced to Granola and Yogurt Cups at the Homestead Restaurant in Charm, Ohio during the early nineties when Lee Ann Miller and I used to sit in one of their restaurant booths and chat over breakfast. I learned a lot about cooking during those years in my friendship with Lee Ann and her mother, Anne. Since then, this breakfast item has become a tradition for weekend breakfasts alongside bacon and eggs. It is a nice touch to place beside each plate, and they look especially pretty in footed stem glasses.*

*This recipe is more about the assembly of ingredients, but to make it as featured here, you can follow two recipes in this cookbook: Maple Granola on page 160, and Blueberry Compote on page 190.*

**Whole yogurt, either vanilla or plain**
**Maple Granola (page 160), or granola of your choice**
***Blueberry Compote (page 190)***

In a transparent glass, cup, or bowl, place a nice puddle of Blueberry Compote. Scoop the yogurt on top of the compote, then sprinkle with Maple Granola. Lastly, add a spoonful of Blueberry Compote to the top. Prepare for your guests to love it. (This is one of my grandson's favorite things for a snack when he comes to visit. He enjoys it in a fancy glass.)

# French Toast

*A great way to use leftover bread, this French Toast is made by dipping pieces of bread into an egg mixture, frying it in a skillet, and then topping it with confectioners' sugar, butter, and maple syrup.*

**3 large eggs**
**1 cup (244g) milk**
**1 tablespoon (13g) pure vanilla extract**
**1 teaspoon (2.6g) ground cinnamon**
**1 pinch salt**
**Confectioners' sugar, for garnish**
**Maple syrup, for serving**
**6–8 thick slices of bread**

In a medium mixing bowl, whip the eggs, milk, vanilla, cinnamon, and salt until blended. Dip the bread slices into the mixture, one at a time, then fry them in a buttered skillet over medium heat, about 4 minutes per side. Cover with a lid while cooking to speed up the process. To serve, garnish with confectioners' sugar and serve with maple syrup.

# Music and Art

*Music and art play an important role at Amish social gatherings and special events. Not many Amish know how to play an instrument, though. They believe that learning an instrument creates a sense of pride and superiority—values that are the exact opposite of their beliefs. Some Amish have learned to play the harmonica or the accordion, but they may not play them publicly, lest they show individuality. They feel the same way about art. They shun certain forms of art, like photography, that show vanity and individualism. However, they embrace other forms of art that honor simplicity, humility, and community, like quilting.*

I first learned of Beethoven's *Symphony No. 5* while crossing the threshold of a tiny art studio in Berlin, Ohio in the late seventies. A somewhat famous German artist, Heinz Gaugel, from the other Berlin, had set up residence to depict the history of the Amish and Mennonites from their Anabaptist beginnings in a 250-foot cyclorama. My curiosity led me there and now, here I was, inside the door. I paused to let my eyes adjust to the bright light as billows of music cascaded around me. Straight ahead perched high on a ladder was the artist, splashing paint on a canvas bigger than life. I shivered, senses stimulated from beauty overload.

My encounter that day with art and music, and, yes, even the artist, with whom I worked for several years, instantly broadened my world. While it deepened my appreciation for the history of our culture, it also caused me to question the relevance of some traditions. Looking back, I am incredibly grateful for this experience and how it helped to shape my path going forward. (You can see Mr. Gaugel's completed work, "Behalt," housed in the Amish Mennonite Heritage Center in Berlin, Ohio.)

A section of the Anabaptist Cyclorama "Behalt" from the Amish Mennonite Heritage Center in Berlin, Ohio.

Oil painting of me in 1979 by Heinz Gaugel.

# Quiltings

*Most Amish quilting bees are held during the winter months when the world is colder and darker and the fields are barren. They began as a practical art to help people stay warm in areas where the winters are harsh. Amish quilts started with dark colors, including purples, greens, browns, and blues, to reflect their simplicity and devotion to God. At first, they were made with a single piece of fabric or scraps of fabric from other quilts, and the quilts were hand sewn. Over time, the Amish quilts became more complex, using patterns and stitches to make their designs unique. Because quilting is a simple and artistic venture, creating unique designs is not considered individualistic—their quilting bees create a community in which the women can gather and visit.*

Once a month, our church's sewing ladies got together for quiltings. As a child, I remember attending every one of these with my mother, until I was of school age and then I could only come along in the summer. There would be several large quilts stretched out in their frames with women seated around each, often 10 women per quilt. Happy chatter and a fair amount of gossip happened around those quilts while delicious lunch smells came from the kitchen. I anticipated a variety of pies and other desserts to satisfy my sweet tooth.

There were also several sewing machines set up where some women were sewing clothes and blankets, which were distributed to needy families. When the quilts were completed, often the same day, they were donated to places like the Haiti Sale or the Mt. Hope Relief Sale where they were auctioned off and the proceeds sent to help relief efforts in foreign countries.

I got my first quilting lessons at these events, and even though I never managed to duplicate my mother's delicate stitches, I did learn how to thread a needle, hold a thimble, and neatly follow the lines of the pattern. And years later, when there were no more quiltings to attend, I often helped my mother work on a quilt of her own. Now, my children each have one of her quilts, and it is a beautiful keepsake to remind them of the wonderful and kind grandmother whose exceptional sewing skills created a work of art.

Amish quilting reflects a legacy of simplicity, community, and craftsmanship that is passed down through generations.

# CHAPTER 7

One of my favorite ways to capture the taste of summer fruit is to make compotes and preserves. Most of us who grew up in the Amish and Mennonite culture remember strawberry freezer jam (Frozen Fresh Strawberry Jam, page 190) and how delicious it was when slathered on freshly baked bread. In fact, many of us probably still make it today. There is something about this jam that preserves the taste of a June summer and brings it right back in the middle of winter.

Mother always made Grape Jam (page 185) or jelly, too, from the abundant harvest of Concord grapes on our farm. And when peaches came into season, she would stand at the stove cooking that golden fruit with sugar to make preserves, which she canned in small jars. And then those jars would be carried to our basement and added as sweet jewels on our canning shelf amidst tomato juice, pickles, red beets, apple sauce, grape juice, and so much more.

It is likely this memory of my mother preserving fruit that sparked my love for doing the same. While I love making jam, I also get immense gratification out of making compotes, which involves cooking chunks of fruit slowly in a sugary syrup until they collapse into jammy puddles. A Blueberry Compote (page 190) or Peach Compote (page 189), for instance, can be used as a topping for pudding or a cream pie. And any compote added between the layers of cake and frosting will elevate the taste. Can you imagine a vanilla cake with creamy Vanilla Buttercream (page 188) and layers of Blackberry Compote (page 189) oozing out when you place a slice on a plate? Or a rich chocolate cake with swirls of Cherry Preserves (page 191) in between the layers?

Just like preserves and compotes capture the taste of a June summer, frostings can also be infused with flavors of the season. In late spring, you can add freshly chopped strawberries or pureed blueberries. In summer, you can add peach juice or grape puree. Fall and winter bring a new variety of flavors such as cinnamon, maple, pumpkin, or chai. And year-round, you can add the delicious taste of melted chocolate, citrus, and even coffee.

I will admit, the only frosting I learned how to make as a teenager was the boiled Maple Frosting (page 188). For all other frosting needs, it was easy to reach for the Betty Crocker can of ready-made. Over time, I tried various recipes for frosting and have landed on American buttercream as my favorite, although it will never replace the maple frosting of my memories. You'll find a variety of recipes here from chocolate, vanilla, and cream cheese to more complex ones like salted caramel or those infused with fruit. And then there's the vintage Chocolate Sour Cream Frosting (page 183) that will have you licking the spoon.

Finally, there is a recipe for Homemade Whipped Cream (page 184), an easy Salted Caramel Sauce (page 178) that seems intimidating at first but is worth the effort, and luscious Lemon Curd (page 182). You will also find sauces, crème fillings, and other things I enjoy using for cakes and desserts.

Over the years, I have come to appreciate that it is the simple things we can make from scratch which add so much flavor to our baking. It literally is the icing on the cake.

## • RECIPES •

# Frostings & Compotes

# How to Make Salted Caramel Sauce

*Caramel may seem intimidating to cook, and there is certainly more than one way to make it, but this is the way I learned. Be patient with yourself, and it may take more than one try if you've never made it before. It is such a delicious treat to use in frostings, on cakes, and over ice cream, and you can store it for several weeks in the refrigerator.*



## Ingredients

1½ cups (300g) white sugar
1½ cups (340.5g) heavy cream, warmed
½ teaspoon (2.84g) coarse salt

**1.** In a heavy bottomed saucepan over medium heat, sprinkle the sugar evenly across the bottom of the pan.

**2.** While the sugar is melting, gently warm the milk (don't boil).

**3.** The sugar will begin to melt slowly, and it's important not to leave the stove during the process. (I have burned too many batches of caramel by thinking I could multitask while the sugar was melting!) If the sugar looks like it is getting too dark before it's all melted, reduce the heat.

**4.** Do not stir the sugar, but you can swirl the pan from time to time for the sugar to melt evenly. This process of melting the sugar takes approximately 10 minutes.

**5.** When the sugar has completely melted and turned an amber color, turn the heat to low and pour the warmed milk into it. Be careful, it will bubble up and act like it's going crazy.

**6.** Let it boil in the pan for about 5 minutes. It will begin to settle into a gentle boil and look more like caramel.

**7.** At the end of 5 minutes, add the salt and pour it into a heatproof bowl. Don't worry about scraping the bottom of the pan too much because you don't want those hardened shards in your bowl of smooth caramel.

**8.** Cool to room temperature and then cover and refrigerate if not using right away. It will thicken as it cools. When you are ready to use it, you can always heat it for about 15–30 seconds in the microwave or on the stovetop on low.

# Raspberry Buttercream

*This frosting uses dehydrated raspberry powder to give it a beautiful pink color and raspberry flavor.*

**2 cups (452g) butter, softened to room temperature**
**4 cups (500g) confectioners' sugar, sifted**
**2 tablespoons (16g) dehydrated raspberry powder***
**2 teaspoons (8.4g) pure vanilla extract**
**1 pinch salt**
**2–4 tablespoons (30.1–61g) milk, warmed (if needed)**

**I like to use the organic Koyah® brand. Alternatively, you can buy dehydrated raspberries (or dehydrate your own) and then grind them into powder in a food processor or blender.*

In the bowl of a stand mixer, beat the butter on medium-high speed for about 6–8 minutes, scraping the bowl periodically. When it has become creamy and light, slowly add the confectioners' sugar, raspberry powder, vanilla, and salt and whip again until fully combined, at least 2 more minutes, scraping the bowl. Lastly, if you would like your frosting to be a bit thinner, add the warmed milk and whip again until it's incorporated. If you would like a stronger raspberry flavor or brighter color, just add more raspberry powder.

# Hot Fudge Sauce

*Elsie Stutzman, Sugarcreek, Ohio*

*This recipe from my sister-in-law is an easy answer to a last-minute dessert. This decadent Hot Fudge Sauce can be ready in about 15 minutes to pour over bowls of ice cream for happy guests.*

**½ cup (113g) butter**
**3 tablespoons (15.93g) cocoa powder**
**One 14-ounce (396g) can Eagle brand milk**
**1 pinch salt**
**½ teaspoon (2.15g) pure vanilla extract**

Melt butter, then stir in cocoa powder, Eagle Brand milk, and salt. Do all this on medium heat, always whisking. Just bring to boiling point—do not boil. Remove from heat and stir in vanilla. Serve warm over ice cream.

# Peanut Butter Frosting

*This frosting is delicious on a chocolate cake. To make it extra fancy, you can garnish the cake with miniature Reese's® Peanut Butter Cups or crushed Reese's Peanut Butter Cups. I also love to use it on Banana Cake (page 58).*

**2 cups (452g) butter, at room temperature**
**¼ cup (62.5g) peanut butter**
**4 cups (454g) confectioners' sugar**
**1 tablespoon (13g) pure vanilla extract**
**1 pinch salt**

In the bowl of a stand mixer, beat the butter until it's soft and fluffy, then blend in the peanut butter and salt, scraping the bowl. Slowly add the confectioners' sugar and the vanilla extract, then beat until well blended.

# Salted Caramel Buttercream

*Delicious on chocolate cake, this frosting will have you licking the bowl.*

**2 cups (452g) unsalted butter, softened**
**4 cups (520g) confectioners' sugar, sifted**
**1 pinch salt**
**1 cup (200g) salted caramel sauce**

In the bowl of a stand mixer, whip the butter until it is soft and fluffy, about 6–8 minutes. Scrape the bowl, reduce the speed, and slowly add the confectioners' sugar. Scrape the bowl from time to time as you whip it thoroughly to combine. Last, add the salt and the caramel sauce and whip again until the frosting is smooth.

FROSTINGS & COMPOTES

# Fresh Strawberry Frosting

*Clara Gingerich Miller, Dover, Delaware*

*This frosting folds the summery taste of strawberries into a buttercream to liven up a cake.*

**1 cup (226g) butter, softened**
**1½ cups (165g) confectioners' sugar**
**½ cup (83.5g) chopped strawberries**
**½ cups (56.5g) nuts (optional)**
**½ cup (32.5g) unsweetened shredded coconut (optional)**

In the bowl of a stand mixer, whip the butter until it is creamy, about 5-8 minutes. Scrape the bowl, then gradually add the confectioners' sugar. Mix thoroughly, then slowly add the strawberries until blended. If using nuts or coconut, fold those in last. This is enough to frost a 9 x 13-inch sheet cake.

# Lemon Curd

*A tart and creamy topping bursting with the flavor of citrus and delicious served on scones, pancakes, cakes, and so much more. It is also yummy when swirled into your favorite yogurt and granola bowl.*

**2 large eggs**
**2 large egg yolks**
**⅔ cup (132g) white sugar**
**Zest of 2 medium lemons**
**Juice of 2-4 medium lemons, at least ½ cup (122g)**
**1 pinch salt**
**6 tablespoons (84.75g) butter, cut up**

In a medium pot, whisk together the eggs and egg yolks. Next, in a small bowl, measure out the sugar and add the lemon zest. Massage the sugar and lemon zest together for a few minutes. Then, add the sugar, lemon zest, and lemon juice to the eggs in the pot. Turn on medium heat and begin whisking briskly and constantly. Mixture will slowly begin to thicken over several minutes. (To get a smooth and creamy curd, the constant whisking is important.) When it reaches the bubbling point, remove from the heat and add the salt and butter. Whisk until blended. If desired, you may strain the curd to remove the zest. Otherwise, cool completely and then cover and refrigerate until ready to use.

# Chocolate Sour Cream Frosting

*An old-fashioned recipe, this tangy frosting made with two ingredients, three if you wish, is finger-licking delicious. Just make sure the sour cream is at room temperature, or the chocolate will seize up when you stir them together.*

**2 cups (340g) semi-sweet chocolate, melted**
**2 cups (500g) sour cream, at room temperature**
**1 tablespoon (15g) maple syrup, at room temperature (optional)**

Bring sour cream to room temperature. You can speed up this process by measuring 2 cups into a Pyrex measuring cup and placing it in a bowl of hot water, stirring from time to time. If you are using maple syrup for additional sweetness, you can add the syrup to the milk. Meanwhile, place the chocolate into a medium bowl placed over a pot of simmering water (the bottom of the bowl should not be touching the water). Stir occasionally, and when the chocolate has melted, remove from the heat. When the sour cream has reached room temperature, pour it into the bowl of melted chocolate and stir quickly to combine, using a small spatula. Continue to stir until you have a smooth, streak-free consistency. If it seems a little too runny, you can leave it set in the bowl for an additional 20 minutes or so before frosting it over a cooled cake.

# Concord Grape Puree

*My father planted grapevines on our farm and growing up I can remember the distinct smell of ripening grapes that came through the screen windows each August. When the grapes were deeply blue the harvest began. Mostly the Concord grapes were used to preserve gallons and gallons of grape juice for the winter months and to make grape jelly for filling pantry shelves. But these days I like to also use them to make a fruity puree for Concord Grape Buttercream (page 185), which I use for cakes.*

**14 ounces (400g) Concord grapes, removed from their stems**
**3 tablespoons (44g) water**
**¼ cup (50g) white sugar**
**1 tablespoon (15g) lemon juice**

Rinse the grapes and remove them from their stems. Place them in a medium-sized saucepan and add the sugar, water, and lemon juice. Stir and bring to a boil. Allow to boil for about 5 minutes to let the skins break open, stirring occasionally. Remove from the stove and pour into a large sieve set over a bowl. With a wooden spoon or spatula, smash the grapes around in the sieve to remove as much of the juice and pulp as possible. Discard the skins and the seeds left in the sieve, then pour the puree back into the saucepan on the stove and boil slowly to reduce for about 5 minutes. This process of reduction will make the flavor more concentrated. Yields about ¾ (184.2g) cup of puree.

# Homemade Whipped Cream

*Once you get used to making homemade whipped cream, it will be hard to use the store-bought variety. It is easy to make with only a few ingredients and the taste is so much better.*

**1 cup (248g) heavy whipping cream**
**¼ cup (28.38g) confectioners' sugar**
**1 pinch salt**
**1 teaspoon (4.3g) pure vanilla extract**

In the bowl of a stand mixer, pour all the ingredients and whip until medium peaks form. You can also whip this by hand using a whisk. Makes about 2 cups.

# Grape Jam

*Esther Miller, Mt. Hope, Ohio*

*Concord grapes grow prolifically throughout Ohio, Pennsylvania, and around some of the Great Lakes. Growing up, we always harvested them in late August and made grape juice and jam. This is an easy jam recipe which you can either store in the freezer or cold pack to make it shelf stable.*

**4 cups (604g) Concord grapes, washed and removed from stems**
**4 cups (800g) white sugar**
**2 tablespoons (29.57g) water**

In a medium-sized pot, add the grapes, sugar, and water. Stir, and then boil for 20 minutes. Cool slightly and then push through a strainer. Fill jam jars, cover with lids and rings. You can either cold pack them for 10 minutes to make them shelf stable or let them rest on the counter for 24 hours and then store them in the freezer. Yields 2 jam jars.

# Concord Grape Buttercream

*This frosting incorporates the familiar childhood taste of Concord grapes harvested in late summer from my father's grapevines on the farm. It also gives the frosting a lavender hue.*

**2 cups (454g) unsalted butter, room temperature**
**4 cups (520g) confectioners' sugar, sifted**
**¾ cup (184.2g) Concord Grape Puree (page 184)***
**1 tablespoon (15g) lemon juice**
**½ teaspoon (3g) sea salt (or more, to taste)**
**2 tablespoons (30g) milk, warmed**

**You can also use ¾ cup of home-canned grape juice, undiluted. The store-bought variety does not carry enough flavor or color.*

In the bowl of a stand mixer, whip the butter until it is creamy and almost fluffy. This will take about 5 minutes (set a timer because it is longer than you think). Scrape the bowl periodically. Add the salt and confectioners' sugar slowly and mix until incorporated. Then, drizzle in the Concord Grape Puree and the lemon juice and whip for several more minutes. Lastly, add the warmed milk and whip again until the frosting is smooth.

# Rosemary Sugared Cranberries

*At Christmas, I love to use these sugared cranberries to decorate cakes, pies, and other desserts.*

**1 cup (100g) fresh cranberries, whole**
**1 sprig fresh rosemary**
**1 cup (200g) white sugar, divided**
**½ cup (119g) water**

In a small pan on the stovetop, heat ½ cup (100g) of sugar with ½ cup (119g) of water and the sprig of rosemary. Heat until it comes to a boil, stirring occasionally. Boil for 1 minute, remove from heat, and allow to steep for a few minutes before removing the sprig of rosemary. Next, dip the cranberries in the syrup and remove them with a slotted spoon, transferring them to a small tray lined with parchment paper. Let them dry on the tray for 1 hour, then roll them in ½ cup (100g) white sugar and allow to rest for another hour on a clean tray. These can be used to decorate cakes and other desserts during the holidays when fresh cranberries are in season.

# Crème Filling

*Made with a combination of Crisco, butter, and marshmallow crème, this vanilla filling is perfect to use for whoopie pies, Ho Hos Snack Cake, chocolate rolls, or to place in between layers of a cake.*

**1 cup (205g) Crisco**
**¼ cup (56.5g) butter, softened at room temperature**
**2½ cups (283.75g) confectioners' sugar, sifted**
**1 cup (238g) marshmallow crème**
**1 teaspoon (4.3g) pure vanilla extract**
**2 pinches salt**
**2 tablespoons (30.5g) milk**

In the bowl of a stand mixer, whip the Crisco and butter until it's fluffy. Scrape the bowl, then add the confectioners' sugar and marshmallow crème, whipping again to combine. Add the vanilla extract, salt, and milk. Then, whip on medium to high speed to fully incorporate for several minutes until the frosting is fluffy.

# Slow-Cooked Apple Butter

*This recipe is from an old cookbook from the Pleasant View Mennonite Church I have been using for many years. It is an easier way of making apple butter than cooking it for a whole day in a copper kettle over an open fire, as I grew up doing with my aunts and uncles.*

**4–5 pounds assorted apples such as Arkansas Black, Macintosh, Cortland, and Jonathan**
**3 cups (600g) white sugar**
**2 teaspoons (5.2g) ground cinnamon**
**½ teaspoon (1.3g) ground cloves**
**½ teaspoon (1.3g) ground allspice**

Wash, core, and quarter the apples. (No need to peel.) There should be enough to fill a medium-to-large crockpot. In a medium bowl, whisk together the sugar and the spices, then pour over the apples and stir. Cover and cook for 3 hours on high. Uncover and stir the apples. Cover and cook for 9 more hours on low. At the end of this time, remove the lid, stir, and, working in small batches, place in a blender and puree for a few seconds until smooth. Ladle into jars with lids and store in refrigerator or freezer or follow a water bath process for canning. If freezing, allow a 1-inch space at the top of the jars. Makes about 4–5 pints.

# Peppermint Buttercream

*This buttercream pairs well with chocolate cake and is also delicious to use as a filling in whoopie pies at Christmas. It looks pretty when garnished with crushed peppermint.*

**2 cups (452g) butter, softened at room temperature**
**4 cups (454g) confectioners' sugar, sifted**
**2 teaspoons (8.4g) pure vanilla extract**
**½ teaspoon (2g) peppermint extract**
**1 pinch salt**
**2–4 tablespoons (30.5g–61g) milk, warmed (if needed)**

In the bowl of a stand mixer, whip the butter for about 5 minutes until it's creamy and fluffy. Slowly add the confectioners' sugar, scraping the bowl. Beat for several minutes to incorporate, then add the vanilla extract, the peppermint extract, and salt. Whip on medium-high speed until fully combined. If frosting is too thick, add 2–4 tablespoons warm milk and whip again.

# Vanilla Buttercream

*Fluffy and light, this buttercream can be used as a base for many other flavors but is also perfect on its own.*

**2 cups (452g) butter, softened to room temperature**
**4 cups (500g) confectioners' sugar, sifted**
**1 tablespoon (13g) pure vanilla extract**
**1 pinch salt**

In the bowl of a stand mixer, beat the butter on medium-high speed for about 6-8 minutes, scraping the bowl periodically. When it has become creamy and light, slowly add the confectioners' sugar, vanilla, and salt, and whip again until fully combined, at least 2 more minutes, scraping the bowl.

# Maple Frosting

*This is the frosting of my childhood which was most often used on cinnamon rolls but is also delicious on fried donuts or chocolate cake. Actually, it's good on anything.*

**2 cups (330g) brown sugar, packed**
**10 tablespoons (141.25g) butter, softened**
**½ teaspoon (2.84g) salt**
**⅔ cup (166g) milk**
**3 cups (330g) confectioners' sugar, sifted**
**1 teaspoon (4g) maple extract (you may also substitute with pure vanilla extract)**

1. Put sugar, butter, and salt into a medium saucepan and cook over medium heat until mixture begins to bubble, stirring constantly. Add milk and boil gently for 1 minute, then remove from heat and cool for about 15 minutes.

2. In bowl of a stand mixer with a whisk attachment, beat the slightly warm mixture with the confectioners' sugar and maple extract until creamy.

*This frosting will set up after it is made, so do not make it until you need to use it. If you have leftovers, you can store the frosting in the fridge in a covered container, and when ready to use, warm it briefly in the microwave until it reaches spreading consistency.*

# Peach Compote

*This compote is made with fresh peaches and can be used as a topping for dessert, cakes, ice cream, or pudding.*

**6 cups (1106g) sliced fresh peaches**
**1 cup (202g) white sugar**
**2 tablespoons (30g) lemon juice**
**2 tablespoons (28g) butter**
**½ cup (117.66g) water**
**5 tablespoons (35g) cornstarch**

Combine peaches, sugar, lemon juice, and butter in a saucepan over medium heat. Meanwhile, make a slurry with the water and the cornstarch. When the peach mixture begins to boil, stir in the cornstarch and water mixture, whisking constantly, until the peach topping turns from cloudy to translucent and shiny. Cool in a bowl.

FROSTINGS & COMPOTES

# Blackberry Compote

*Made with fresh blackberries, this is a delicious topping for dessert, ice cream, or pudding. It can also be used as a filling for hand pies.*

**2 pints fresh blackberries, about 2½-3 cups (360g)**
**¼ cup (58.83g) water**
**⅓ cup (67.33g) white sugar**
**1 pinch salt**
**1 tablespoon (7g) cornstarch**
**Juice of 1 lemon (about 2 tablespoons or 30g)**

Heat the berries, water, sugar, and salt on the stovetop until the berries soften and release their juices. Make a slurry with the lemon juice and cornstarch, then stir into the blackberry mixture. Stir constantly until mixture thickens, bubbles, and turns clear. Remove from heat and cool completely.

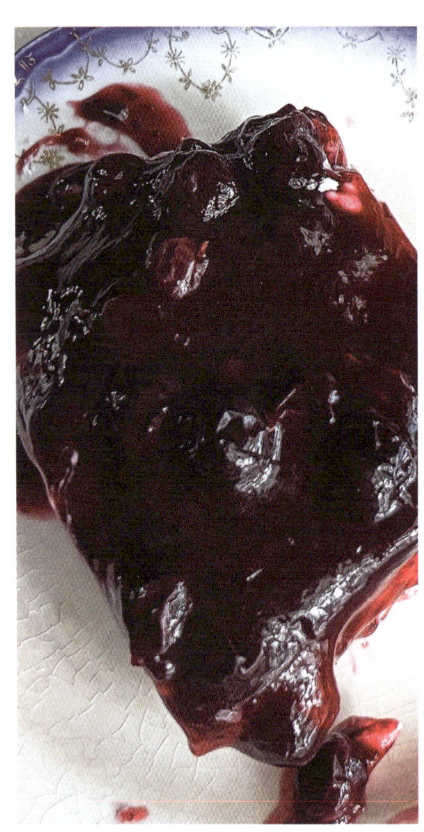

# Blueberry Compote

*Made with fresh blueberries, this compote can be used as a topping for cakes and desserts or as a filling for hand pies.*

**4 cups (600g) fresh blueberries**
**½ cup (117.66g) water**
**2 tablespoons (11.25g) cornstarch**
**2 tablespoons (29.58g) water**
**⅔ cup (132g) white sugar**
**Juice and grated rind of 1 lime or lemon (approximately 2 tablespoons or 30 g juice)**
**¼ teaspoon (1.4g) salt**
**1 tablespoon (14.13g) unsalted butter**

In a medium saucepan, heat the blueberries with ½ cup water until they begin to burst, approximately 5 minutes. Meanwhile, in a small bowl, make a slurry with the cornstarch, 2 tablespoons water, lime or lemon juice, and sugar, whisking until no lumps remain. Add the slurry to the bubbling blueberries on the stove and whisk constantly until mixture thickens and starts to boil. Allow to bubble for about 1 minute, then remove from heat and whisk in the butter and zest. Pour into a bowl to cool.

# Frozen Fresh Strawberry Jam

*Esther Miller*

*This is the basic recipe on the Sure Jell® box for strawberry freezer jam—the quantities have just been increased. This is a family favorite, and my children request it every year. The strawberry flavor shines brightly since the berries are not cooked.*

**4 cups (approximately 940–980g) crushed strawberries**
**8 cups (1600g) white sugar**
**1½ cups (354.88g) water**
**Two 1.75-ounce (49g) boxes Sure Jell**

Stir fresh strawberries and sugar together in a large mixing bowl. Bring water and Sure Jell to a boil on stovetop, stirring constantly. Boil for 1 minute, then pour into the strawberry mixture and whisk or stir for 3 minutes until the sugar has dissolved completely. Pour into jelly jars and cover with lids. Let the jars set on the counter for 24 hours, then place them in the freezer until you are ready to use. Yields about 5–6 pint jars or 8–10 jam jars.

# Cherry Preserves

*Using sweet red cherries, this recipe is delicious in between layers of chocolate cake with chocolate buttercream. And, of course, it is always great with homemade bread or biscuits.*

**4 cups (620g) fresh or frozen, pitted dark red cherries, divided**
**¾ cup (150g) white sugar, plus 1 tablespoon (12.38g)**
**1 tablespoon (15g) lemon juice**
**1 teaspoon (2g) lemon zest**
**1 pinch salt**

In a medium mixing bowl, measure out 3 cups of cherries. Chop them up, then add 1 cup of whole cherries into the bowl of chopped cherries. Stir in the sugar, lemon juice, lemon zest, and salt, and let it rest on the counter for about 30 minutes until the cherries start to get juicy. Then, pour into a medium saucepan and bring to a boil on the stove. Boil gently for about 20–25 minutes, stirring frequently. Watch closely so it does not boil over or stick to the bottom. You can tell the preserves are done when the mixture has been greatly reduced and the liquid becomes more syrup-like. Remove from heat and pour into a bowl to cool, then refrigerate until ready to use. This makes approximately 1½ cups of preserves.

# Sour Cherry Compote

*Slightly tart, this cherry compote goes well as a filling for layer cakes, or as a topping for vanilla pudding. I have also used it to add a bit of color and sweetness to yogurt and granola breakfast bowls, or as a filling for hand pies.*

**2 cups (308g) sour cherries, pitted and drained (save juice)**
**½ cup (134.5g) sour cherry juice**
**⅓ cup (66g) white sugar**
**2 tablespoons (30g) lemon juice**
**1 pinch salt**
**2 tablespoons (30g) water**
**1 tablespoon (8g) cornstarch**
**½ teaspoon (2.1g) pure vanilla extract**

In a medium-sized baking pot, bring the cherries, juice, sugar, lemon juice, and salt to a boil. Boil slowly for about 3-5 minutes, then make a slurry with the water and cornstarch and pour into the boiling cherries. Stir constantly. Mixture will turn from cloudy to translucent. When the mixture is shiny and bubbling again, remove from the heat and add vanilla extract. Cool to room temperature, then place in the refrigerator until ready to serve.

# My Family and Scenes from Our Amish Country Home

## (Holmes County, Ohio)

One of the vegetable gardens of Cousin Esther's farm with their buggy horses in the pasture beyond.

Buggies parked at the hitching rail where their owners are shopping at the Walnut Creek Cheese store in Berlin, Ohio.

My daughter and business partner, Natalie.

A family built on love and cinnamon rolls.

This was Dan and Aunt Elizabeth Troyer's farm in Mt. Hope, Ohio, which has now been passed down to her daughter Esther and her husband Larry Miller who continue in the Amish faith and traditions of our ancestors.

# Acknowledgments

For years people have been telling me I should write a cookbook, but the undertaking seemed huge. Especially in the middle of building a business from scratch and the day-to-day care of helping it grow. But then one day I received an email from Fox Chapel Publishing in Lancaster, Pennsylvania with an invitation to work on a collection of Amish and Mennonite recipes for a new edition in their series of cookbooks. Thus began a relationship with my competent editor, Christine Savicky, and publisher, Alan Giagnocavo.

Christine, thank you for believing in my ability to handle this project. I can't imagine someone more kind or helpful to have had by my side through this journey. You made it possible to complete this task by giving me extra time when I needed it and have been so encouraging every step of the way. And Alan, I enjoyed the Zoom® chats we had discussing similarities between the Amish of Ohio and Pennsylvania and enjoyed learning of your growing up in Canada. Thank you for taking me on for this project.

Thank you to my husband and family who understood that family dinners would be eaten amidst piles of recipes cluttering the dining room. And that takeout meals might be on the menu, though there was always scratch-made dessert. Through it all, you cheered me on and told me how proud you were of me. I love you more than anything.

To my team at the bakery, and my daughter, Natalie—thank you for often carrying on without me and for helping me test some of the recipes when I was running out of time. I appreciate you all so much.

To my extended family who submitted recipes, thank you for sharing a part of your lives with me. I am honored to feature the recipes you've used in your families for so long.

A big thank you to Lauren Olinger of Red Cardinal Studio for the portrait photos. Since 2014, you have been documenting my journey in food in all kinds of weather, climbing ladders, moving furniture, always looking for the best angle. You are the best.

And a huge thanks to my assistant, Lee Bottoms, who gussied up my iPhone photos, took on countless hours of editing, and helped with photography when needed. You were a huge help with the technical aspect of this book, and I appreciate you so much.

Handwritten recipes from my mother's kitchen.

# About the Author

Naomi Stutzman Gingerich is a freelance writer, storyteller, and entrepreneur raised in the simplistic lifestyle of the Plain People. She grew up on a dairy farm in Holmes County, Ohio's Amish Country, the youngest of five in a Mennonite home. With a father who was ordained as a Deacon, later a Minister, and then a Bishop by lot in the Conservative Mennonite Conference, and a mother who was a homemaker and an excellent baker, Naomi learned the nuances of church, farming, and cooking in the context of family at a young age and looks back fondly on the values with which she was raised.

At 17, she met internationally known artist, Heinz Gaugel (1927-2000) during his painting of the cyclorama known as "Behalt." While very unusual for a Mennonite teen, Gaugel commissioned Naomi to work for him in his studio, narrating the story of the Amish and Mennonite heritage from the early days of Anabaptism in Europe to the present-day communities in the United States. This season with Gaugel gave her a greater understanding and appreciation of her Mennonite upbringing, but also caused her to evaluate her own encounter with faith.

Although Naomi left the Mennonite church at age 23, she has carried on many of the traditions of her heritage, which include an emphasis on family and gathering around the table for dinner. Her travels have taken her around the United States, Europe, and Central and South America, and have given her an appreciation for food of all cultures. In 2017, she and her oldest daughter established a bakery café, Louie and Honey's Kitchen, where they share many of the baked goods reminiscent of the Amish and Mennonite culture.

Naomi lives in Winston-Salem, North Carolina with her husband, Fred. Together, they have three children, a son-in-law, a daughter-in-law, and three grandchildren.

# Index